What
"Left Behind"
Left Behind

Dwight K. Nelson

REVIEW AND HERALD® PUBLISHING ASSOCIATION
HAGERSTOWN, MARYLAND

HART BOOKS
A Ministry of Hart Research Center
FALLBROOK, CALIFORNIA

Unless otherwise noted, Bible texts in this book are from the *New Revised Standard Version* of the Bible, copyright © 1989 by the Division of Christian Education of the National Council of the Churches of Christ in the U.S.A. Used by permission.

Scripture quotations marked NASB are from the *New American Standard Bible,* copyright © 1960, 1962, 1963, 1968, 1971, 1972, 1973, 1975, 1977, 1994 by The Lockman Foundation. Used by permission.

Texts credited to NIV are from the Holy Bible, *New International Version.* Copyright © 1973, 1978, 1984, International Bible Society. Used by permission of Zondervan Bible Publishers.

Texts credited to NKJV are from the *New King James Version.* Copyright © 1979, 1980, 1982 by Thomas Nelson, Inc. Used by permisssion. All rights reserved.

Editing and page design by Ken McFarland
Cover art direction and design by Mark Bond, Mark Bond Design

The book and series title ***Left Behind*** is copyrighted and trademark protected by Tyndale House Publishers, Inc., Wheaton, Illinois

The author assumes full responsibility for the accuracy of all facts, quotations, and references as cited in this book.

ISBN: 0-8280-1641-0

Contents

Foreword

WE LIVE IN A BIBLICALLY illiterate world, do we not? A world that has absolutely no clue that Jesus is coming soon.

Leonard Sweet, in his sometimes outrageous but usually provocative book *Soul Tsunami: Sink or Swim in New Millennium Culture,* tells of a pastoral staff in Columbus, Ohio, who headed over to Indianapolis for the annual American sports ritual, March Madness—the NCAA college basketball playoffs. No sooner had the pastors found their seats in the crowded sports arena than they noticed him sitting under the basket at the other end of the court. You've seen him, too, haven't you? Omnipresent at nationally televised sporting events, he's the funny-looking guy with the orange and green hair and a home-made "John 3:16" cardboard sign that he keeps holding up whenever the television cameras pan his way. (He must have a houseful of cousins—how else do you explain the appearances of this ubiquitous "witness for Jesus" simultaneously at sporting events across the land?) The pastors spotted him. So did two well-dressed couples sitting right behind the pastors.

When you're jammed into a sports arena, it isn't hard to eavesdrop on the conversation behind you. The couples were debating the meaning of this most unusual sign: "j-o-h-n-3-colon-1-6," one of them spelled it aloud to the rest. Maybe it's a new restaurant here in Indianapolis, someone suggested. The idea seemed plausible, until another dissed the idea—who would advertise anything of worth using a guy with orange and green hair and a homemade sign? (A lesson, perhaps, to all of us Christians.) Hey, I got it, came another quip. Maybe it's a signal to someone to meet him at the John on the third floor, stall 16. As Leonard Sweet exclaims, "Talk about clueless. They were totally in the dark why anyone would be holding a sign with those words on it."[1]

We live in a biblically illiterate world. Which means it wouldn't be prudent or polite to assume anybody's knowledge of the Bible verse on that homemade sign—"For God so loved the world that he gave his only Son, so that everyone who believes in him may not perish but may have eternal life."[2] It is a biblically illiterate world, but the sign is still right—God loves it!

George Barna reported on a national survey of college students, wherein 20 percent of the respondents answered the question, "Who was Joan of Arc?" with "the wife of Noah"!

We live in a biblically illiterate world and nation, do we not? This postmodern culture is now being described as post-Christian. So how are we going to tell this world that the world is about to end—that Jesus is coming soon? If the words of Jesus in John 3:16 mean nothing more than the third-floor john, then how could they ever grasp His promise in John 14:1-3?

"Do not let your hearts be troubled. Believe in God, believe also in me. In my Father's house are many dwelling places. If it were not so, would I have told you that I go to prepare a place for you? And if I go and prepare a place for you, *I will come again* and will take you to myself, so that where I am, there you may be also."

How in the world are you going to get the world to believe the beloved John 14 promise of Christ: "I will come again"?

Somebody is trying. In what may go down as one of the greatest marketing coups of modern Christianity, not to mention modern fiction, two Christian authors (one a minister, the other a professional writer), together with a team of marketers, may have pulled it off! For they have taken the grand promise of Scripture that Jesus is coming soon and wrapped and woven it into a set of "end-time novels" and offered it all to the biblically illiterate public.

And the public response has broken records! Number one on the *New York Times* best-seller list—number one on the *Wall Street Journal* bestseller list—number one for *USA Today*—number one for *Amazon.com*. And according to Barnes and Noble, their first "end-time novel" became one of the top ten best-sellers of the twentieth century! And now in the twenty-first century, the books keep coming, and the novels keep selling. Eight titles now have become the biggest one-series seller in the history of books! And there are still four more titles to go.

It all began with their first end-time novel, entitled *Left Behind*. Today the world is beating a track to these "second coming" thrillers!

A friend of mine was flying from the east coast to Los Angeles last summer, when with good fortune he was bumped up into first class. Turns out most of the first class was headed to the Democratic Party's presidential convention in Los Angeles. The passengers were mostly all politicians and government leaders. And as my friend visited with them, nearly to a man they were all talking about the book they were reading—*Left Behind*.

I pastor on a university campus. And campuses across the nation have been swept up in the *Left Behind* fascination. Here's a story from *Christian Reader,* a trade magazine for publishers—this particular issue reporting the runaway best-seller:

"Emily Johnston, a college sophomore, wasn't seeking salvation. She just wanted to read a novel that a classmate had lent to her.

"So on a cool night in October 1998, the aspiring artist from Charlotte, North Carolina, settled into her dorm room at Sweetbriar College, planning to skim the prologue to *Left Behind*.

Then she would study for two exams scheduled for the day.

"By sunrise, she hadn't completed a lick of her studies, but she *had* finished the 468-page end-times novel. At breakfast, she told her astonished friend that she was going out that day to buy the second book.

"And to the eternal delight of her friend, Emily announced she now knew Jesus."[3]

My daughter Kristin and I returned from a trip to Australia and a youth congress down under in January. *Left Behind* certainly hasn't been left behind below the equator!

Given the phenomenal publishing success of this international best-selling series of books, was anybody surprised when the first book of the series was transformed into a $17 million movie production? "Left Behind" debuted first as a best-selling video in the fall of 2000. And the producers hoped against hope that a national theater release of the movie would draw in 57 million Americans, according to their *leftbehind-themovie.com* website. Hollywood's record for simultaneous showings across the nation is a reported 3,200 theaters. The "Left Behind" producers were reportedly hoping for a 3,800 opening night record-breaker when the movie was released on February 2, 2001.

What we have witnessed, and no doubt will continue to observe, is arguably the most sophisticated, high-tech marriage of book and screen and computer in the history of Christianity. And all of it for the promotion of the soon return of Jesus Christ!

At the end of the "Left Behind" video is a collage of dramatic scenes from the movie, pieced together for a music video presentation of a song entitled, "The Midnight Cry." Those three words are in fact a phrase very familiar to the spiritual descendants of William Miller, whose 1840s American revival eventually came to be known as the Midnight Cry movement. As I watched the "Left Behind" rendition of "The Midnight Cry," I thought to myself: "And here *we* call ourselves '*Adventists*'— believers in the imminent return of Jesus Christ to this earth.

Yet . . . true to form . . . once again . . . someone else picks up the ball and runs with it."

Only this time—alas—they picked up the wrong ball! Because the ball that got picked up—and the ball they're running with—is riddled with gaping biblical holes.

So much so—and I say this without any malice or judgment, but with deep Christian concern—that the theological and biblical holes in "Left Behind" are truly gaping ones. So much so that if a biblically illiterate Christian or non-Christian accepts the mistaken Bible interpretation offered in these novels—why, even if a biblically *literate* Christian accepts the false premises of the series without examining the evidence in the Bible—that man, that woman, that young adult will end up being the one who is tragically "left behind" in the end!

You see, in the nomenclature of this best-selling series, the two words "left behind" stand for all of those who missed out on Jesus' "secret rapture" coming—which is the major premise of this novel series. According to the novels—and a very popular brand of evangelical theology today—Jesus comes secretly to earth and whisks His saints (all the truly saved Christians of the church) away from earth to heaven. In one split second, they are gone. Nothing left but the clothes they were wearing—left in a heap with their jewelry and accessories. All babies (in utero or newborn), all children, and all true Christians are raptured from the earth before the terrible seven-year tribulation begins with the signing of a covenant with Israel by a United Nations leader who eventually becomes the dreaded Antichrist and rules the world from a newly rebuilt Babylon in the Iraqi desert.

It may sound preposterous, but I must tell you that in the context of a twisting subplot within the books, the reader is propelled from volume to volume.

So, what are you going to say when the people you work with or go to school with or live next door to come up to you and ask, "Hey, what do *you* think about 'Left Behind'? Is Jesus really coming?

And is that really how you Christians believe the world is going to end?" When you're asked by one of the millions of Americans who have read the books or may have seen the movie, "You're an Adventist, are you? Well, what do you believe?"—what are you going to say in response?

Can you fulfill Peter's compelling summons: "Always be prepared to give an answer to everyone who asks you to give the reason for the hope that you have."[4]

Now that the soon coming of Jesus has made it to the top of the bestseller lists and headlines, isn't it time you and I became prepared to give an intelligent, logical, cogent, gracious, hope-filled answer to the queries of the biblically illiterate world in which we live and work and play?

For that reason this book, which began as a series of sermons I preached in the Pioneer Memorial Church on the campus of Andrews University this year, has been prepared for you.[5] So that you might "give the reason for the hope that you have" to anyone who asks. A truly blessed hope that is *not* riddled with theological and biblical holes. For "we did not follow cleverly invented stories . . . about the power and coming of our Lord Jesus Christ."[6]

For that reason too it is imperative that you understand what "Left Behind" has in fact left behind—both biblically and theologically. The chapters that follow will reveal that what this bestselling book series and movie production left behind includes the following:

◆ the most urgent truth of all

◆ the greatest truth of all

◆ the most clarifying truth of all

◆ the most dangerous truth of all

◆ the most compelling truth of all

◆ the most shaking truth of all.

"But what's the big deal?" you ask. "Who cares what our neighbors believe, as long as they believe?" Because, my friend, if they miss what "Left Behind" left behind, they themselves will tragically be left behind in the end. The issues are *that* critical.

"Come now, and let us reason together" is God's invitation to both intellectual inquiry and integrity.[7] And so we must. Reason together. And by the end of this investigation, you'll have six study guides to assist you in giving to all a reason for the hope that you embrace—for the Christ that you follow.

For without that reason, how can we ever pray the Bible's last prayer with passionate confidence?

"Even so, come, Lord Jesus."[8]

Dwight K. Nelson
Berrien Springs, Michigan
Spring, A.D. 2001

Notes:

[1] Leonard Sweet, *Soul Tsunami*, p. 45.

[2] John 3:16.

[3] *Christian Reader*, November/December 1999, pp. 23, 24.

[4] 1 Peter 3:15, NIV.

[5] The sermon series is available at our two websites: *pmchurch.org* (audio) and *rusearching.com* (video)—the latter site is designed to be shared with your friends outside your church.

[6] 2 Peter 1:16, NIV.

[7] Isaiah 1:18, KJV.

[8] Revelation 22:20, KJV.

What "Left Behind" Did Not Leave Behind

REMEMBER THE "don't throw the baby out with the bathwater" adage? Name me one mother in the world who ever did! Although . . .

I was reading Philip Gulley's delightful book *Front Porch Tales,* in which he recalls the day he and his four siblings, along with Mom and Dad, were on vacation and stopped to eat at a Stuckey's. When the family piled back into the car and drove off, young Philip was in the bathroom. Twenty miles down the road, someone counted heads and discovered the omission! As Gulley describes it, they "Took a quick vote to come back for me. It was almost a tie, but at the last minute Mom changed her mind."[1] But still, that's hardly the same as throwing your baby out with the bathwater!

Which is why it's vital that before we take on and tackle the six great truths "Left Behind" has left behind, we pause for a very important moment and remember the truth "Left Behind" *did not* leave behind. Because in our exuberance to defend the truth and correct the errors about the second and soon coming of Jesus, wouldn't it be sad if we forgot to affirm and celebrate the shining good news that's at the heart of it all? Forget to do that, and we would be truly throwing out the Baby (of Bethlehem) with the bathwater!

So let the record be clear that what "Left Behind" *didn't* leave behind is the shining and resplendent truth that *Jesus, the Saviour of the world, is coming soon.* Hallelujah!

> Our gyrating stock markets, our fragile and jittery economies, our bullet-strewn school yards, our hoof-and-mouth and mad-cow cattle, our crescendoing earthquakes, our global meteorological upheavals—the exhausted headlines of earth long ago gave up trying to keep up with the moral and ecological and economic unraveling that has become standard fare around the planet these days. Holy Scripture left a litany of apocalyptic headlines that were to be the harbingers for a final generation's alert and warning. In the words of Christ himself, "Now when these things begin to take place, stand up and raise your heads, because your redemption is drawing near."[2]

Jesus, the Saviour of the world, is coming soon! "Left Behind" *did not* leave that glorious truth behind.

> Do not let your hearts be troubled. Trust in God; trust also in me. In my Father's house are many rooms; if it were not so, I would have told you. I am going there to prepare a place for you. And if I go and prepare a place for you, *I will come back* and take you to be with me that you also may be where I am.[3]

Good News—Or Bad News?

We have His word on it. Jesus, the Saviour of the world, is coming soon. Whether that's good news or bad news, of course, depends on your perspective.

One night this winter, my wife, Karen, and I, along with some friends, set out on a moonlight walk through the snow to nearby Rosehill Cemetery. The night sky was cloudless and crystalline, the air frigid and still. And awash as it was with the silver beams of a full winter moon, the cemetery—at least for that night—shimmered in the night light as a place of frozen beauty. Stone crosses and granite headstones lifted through the snowy blanket atop their beds, casting long, silver shadows upon the white. How many times have the heartbroken in my parish made their winding, mournful way to this village resting place? For them, for you and me, who cling to His promise that "I am the resurrection and the life,"[4] is the soon coming of Jesus to this world good news or bad news? Why bother even to ask!

On the other hand, for the seven Texas penitentiary escapees who on that same winter's night were on the lam from the law, you can be assured that they had absolutely no desire to come face to face with the sheriff posses who were hunting them down! Who wants to meet the Lawgiver when you're running from the law? The sixth chapter of the Apocalypse dramatically portrays earth inhabitants who cry to the rocks to hide them from the face of the returning Saviour. Obviously, whether the soon return of Jesus Christ is good news or bad news depends entirely on your perspective.

A Soul-deep Heaven-longing

But gaze on the full-paletted artistry of a Nathan Greene, whose brushes and canvases have captured a rainbow heaven heretofore only fleetingly glimpsed in our dreams—and how can you not long for the fulfillment of Jesus' promise, "Where I am, you may be also"?[5] Journey into the soul-stirring word and thought pictures of a C. S. Lewis, who with the skill of a bard plucks the strings of a heaven-longing deep within us—and why wouldn't the soon return of Jesus be the very, very best of news for all the earth?

Recognizing the heaven-longing that Jesus' return will one day fill to the full, C. S. Lewis wondered why we weren't more preoccupied with such good news:

> If we consider the unblushing promises of reward and the staggering nature of the rewards promised in the Gospels, it would seem that our Lord finds our desires, not too strong, but too weak. We are half-hearted creatures, fooling about with drink and sex and ambition when infinite joy is offered us. We are like an ignorant child who wants to go on making mud pies in a slum because

he cannot imagine what is meant by the offer of a holiday at the sea. We are far too easily pleased.[6]

We are, aren't we, "far too easily pleased"? Could that be why God's offer of a holiday at the sea of eternity upon the return of Christ can't seem to drag us away from our silly little mud pies? "Far too easily pleased" are we? Or do we yet recognize that haunting and beating deep inside—this yearning for something, somewhere, more? As Lewis wrote: "If I find in myself desires which nothing in this world can satisfy, the only logical explanation is that I was made for another world."

"Let not your heart be troubled. . . . I will come again."[7]

Thanks to the John 3:16 promise that God still holds high on His homemade signboard of the cross, the John 14:1-3 promise is the greatest news this third-millennium world is dying to hear! The Jesus of Calvary still cries out, "Come to Me, and I will give you rest."[8] Come to Me, and your sins are forgiven. Come to Me, . . . and your guilt is cleansed. Come to Me, and your penalty is paid, your death is conquered, your future is guaranteed, your life is eternal. Come to Me. Why would you die, O child of earth? Come to Me, for I am coming for you.

Soon.

Are You Ready?

A memory that becomes more precious to me with each day that passes is the memory of my father preaching when I was a boy. And oh, how my dad could preach! I admired him then, and I do even more today—though Dad has begun that long descent into Alzheimer's. I don't know how many times my father would come to the end of his sermon somewhere in another little church in Japan, and invite my mother to step to the front and sing a gospel invitation. And I can still hear her voice earnestly appealing through the words of that old Roy Pendleton gospel song, "Are You Ready for Jesus to Come?"

Somehow, it seems the right question to ask here at the outset of this journey into the truth about our soon-coming Saviour. There's no point in throwing the Baby out with the bathwater, no point in becoming so preoccupied with defining the wrong and defending the truth that we forget to follow the One who declared, "*I am* the way, and *the truth,* and the life."[9]

The truth is: *Jesus* is the very best news we must never, ever leave behind.

"Are you ready for Jesus to come?" is really the invitation to step into the embrace of His forever friendship every day and every night *until* He comes. It's that simple. Which is why I hope you'll join me—before you turn another page—in turning my mother's appeal into the song of a personal commitment to the Saviour who's coming back.

Soon.

Which is why *now* is the best time to pray the Bible's last prayer.

"Even so, come, Lord Jesus."

Notes

[1]Philip Gulley, *Front Porch Tales,* pp. 68, 69.

[2]Luke 21:28.

[3]John 14:1-3, NIV, emphasis supplied.

[4]John 11:25.

[5]John 14:3, NKJV.

[6]C. S. Lewis, *The Weight of Glory,* p. 4.

[7]John 14:1, 3, KJV.

[8]Matthew 11:28.

[9]John 14:6, emphasis supplied.

The Most Urgent Truth of All

PICTURE THE SCENE. Captain Rayford Steele—tall, dark, and debonair—has just stepped out of his 747 cockpit. It is midnight on this trans-Atlantic flight he is piloting. A nominal churchgoer who has grown tired of his wife's Christianity, Captain Steele has flirted with the attractive blond senior flight attendant, Hattie Durham, who is overseeing cabin service on tonight's flight to London. Leaving his co-pilot in command, Steele no sooner steps out of his dimly lighted cockpit than Hattie Durham literally grabs him.

Read the scene for yourself from the runaway best-seller *Left Behind:*

> As he opened the cockpit door, Hattie Durham nearly bowled him over.
>
> "No need to knock," he said. "I'm coming."
>
> The senior flight attendant pulled him into the galleyway, but there was no passion in her touch. Her fingers felt like talons on his forearm, and her body shuddered in the darkness.
>
> "Hattie?"
>
> She pressed him back against the cooking compartments, her face close to his.

Had she not been clearly terrified, he might have enjoyed this and returned her embrace. Her knees buckled as she tried to speak, and her voice came in a whiny squeal.

"People are missing," she managed to whisper, burying her head in his chest.

He took her shoulders and tried to push her back, but she fought to stay close. "What do you mean?"

She was sobbing now, her body out of control. "A whole bunch of people, just gone!"

"Hattie, this is a big plane. They've wandered to the lavs or someplace."

She pulled his head down so she could speak directly into his ear. Despite her weeping, she was plainly fighting to make herself understood. "I've been everywhere. I'm telling you, dozens of people are missing."

"Hattie, it's still dark. We'll find them."

"I'm not crazy! See for yourself! All over the plane, people have disappeared."

"It's a joke. They're hiding, trying to—"

"Ray! Their shoes, their socks, their clothes, everything was left behind. These people are gone!"[1]

Did you catch those frantic words: "Ray! Their shoes, their socks, their clothes, everything was left behind. These people are gone!" In the movie/video dramatization of this fictitious scene, the camera pans the airplane cabin, revealing little piles of empty clothes lying atop vacant airplane seats. And with that scene begins the saga of those who were "left behind."

Is this the way Christ's second coming will transpire? Does the Bible teach that when Jesus comes to earth the second time He will return secretly, stealthfully, and whisk His closest followers away—leaving the rest of the billions of earth's inhabitants to suffer through a terrible seven-year tribulation? Is there a shred of credible biblical evidence to substantiate what millions of people on earth are being taught, some for the first time, as they read the novels and watch the movie?

In short, *is the secret rapture true?*

Come and explore what "Left Behind" has in fact left behind: the most urgent truth of all.

I am certain that if you approached either of the authors (who I'm sure are godly, devout men)—Tim LaHaye and Jerry Jenkins— or inquired of one of the professors at a large seminary in Texas that officially teaches this theory—that to a man or woman they would urge you to "go to the Bible" and seek your answers there. And so we must. Because what matters is not what I think or you believe or they teach. What matters is, What says the Word of God? So why not open your Bible and follow along as we examine the three key passages these sincere and devout Christians believe are critical to their theory of the "secret rapture."

One Taken—The Other Left

The anchor text of the rapture theory is found in these words of Jesus recorded in Matthew 24:

> But about that day and hour no one knows, neither the angels of heaven, nor the Son, but only the Father. For as the days of Noah were, so will be the coming of the Son of Man. For as in those days before the flood they were eating and drinking, marrying and giving in marriage, until the day Noah entered the ark, and they knew nothing until the flood came and swept them all away, so too will be the coming of the Son of Man. Then two will be in the field; one will be taken and one will be left. Two women will be grinding meal together; one will be taken and one will be left. Keep awake therefore, for you do not know on what day your Lord is coming.[2]

In this passage Jesus describes the human saga just before His return as going through the normal rounds of daily human existence: eating, drinking, and marrying. Nothing wrong with those activities. We do them every day (except for the marrying, of course!).

It is from Jesus' description of the daily rounds of "two in the field" and "two women grinding" (Luke's account of this teaching adds "two in bed")[3] that the "Left Behind" secret rapture series of novels draws its title. The "love scene" in both the book and the movie has Rayford Steele rushing home to Chicago from his aborted trans-Atlantic flight, only to discover beneath the thrown-back bed covers his wife's nightie, her cross necklace and her wedding ring—all left behind when she was raptured in the night. She was taken, and now he is "left behind."

But is that what Jesus is teaching here? Does Matthew 24 in fact corroborate "the secret rapture" theory—i.e., that Christ will come secretly "as a thief in the night" and steal His true followers away?

No, no, no!

Matthew 24 is the great apocalyptic chapter of the gospels, and true to form, it is replete with prophetic warnings and signs straight from the lips and heart of Christ Himself. Let me share with you three reasons Matthew 24 cannot and does not support the "secret rapture" theory.

Don't Believe It!

Reason #1—Jesus warns against anyone teaching that His coming will be in secret:

> Then if anyone says to you, "Look! Here is the Messiah!" or "There he is!"—*do not believe it.* For false messiahs and false prophets will appear and produce great signs and omens, to lead astray, if possible, even the elect. Take note, I have told you beforehand. So, if they say to you, "Look! He is in the wilderness," do not go out. If they say, "Look! He is in the inner rooms," *do not believe it.*[4]

Note it carefully: twice Jesus powerfully warns against any teaching that would suggest He would come secretly or stealthfully. "Do not believe it . . . do not believe it." No matter how persuasively the theory is taught, no matter how powerfully the story is told—Jesus is unequivocal: "Do not believe it."

Then if You're not returning secretly, Lord, what will Your second coming be like? "For as the lightning comes from the east and flashes as far as the west, so will be the coming of the Son of Man."[5]

Have you ever tried to sleep through a lightning storm? We have some humdinger springtime thunderstorms here in Michigan! Whenever Karen and I awaken to one of those rumbling midnight explosions, we commence the "one lollipop, two lollipop" count routine. It has nothing to do with being hungry. Rather, it's that we're nervously trying to gauge the time span between the bedroom-illuminating white flash of light and the crashing thunder. What really gets your hair standing straight on end is when the white light and the exploding thunder are simultaneous! You've just been struck. You may smile, but Karen's brother's house in Indianapolis burned down when it was struck by lightning.

Nobody sleeps through a lightning and thunderstorm. *It is no secret.* And that, Jesus declared, is how My return to earth will be. So "do not believe" anyone who tries to tell you I am coming secretly.

And as if anyone could still be in doubt about how "un-secret" His second coming will be, Jesus then graphically depicts its spectacular character:

> Then the sign of the Son of Man will appear in heaven, and then all the tribes [*nations,* NIV] of the earth will mourn, and they will see 'the Son of Man coming on the clouds of heaven' with power and great glory. And he will send out his angels with a loud trumpet call, and they will gather his elect from the four winds, from one end of heaven to the other.[6]

Matthew's IMAX

Have you ever sat spellbound in a surround-sound, eight-stories-tall giant-screen IMAX theater? The sound is so wall-vibratingly vibrant, and the screen is so massive, it's as if you were there in the Grand Canyon or inside that spinning stunt plane or atop the space shuttle or . . . and the list goes on and on. Because there's one reality about IMAX—it's the next-best thing to being there!

Matthew opens up a towering IMAX screen for us here in chapter 24, as the heavens explode with "power and glory" (the Greek word for "power" is the very one our word "dynamite" comes from)! Taller than eight stories, Matthew's canvas literally fills every millimeter of the fiery sky with the returning Jesus and a few trillion angels! And the sound effects? Why, not even a million surround-sound speakers would do justice to that glorious event.

A secret coming? Hardly! Jesus is unequivocal in His warning: If anyone tells you I have come in secret, "do not believe it!"

Ringside Seats for the Main Event

Reason #2 as to why Matthew cannot and does not support the "secret rapture" theory—Jesus declares that the whole world will witness His return.

He couldn't be more plain:

> Then the sign of the Son of Man will appear in heaven, and then *all* the tribes [*nations,* NIV] of the earth will mourn, and *they will see* 'the Son of Man coming on the clouds of heaven' with power and great glory.[7]

Could Jesus be more plain? *All* the nations of earth will *witness* the second coming of Jesus Christ. Jesus Himself has declared that reality. Contrary to the teaching of *Left Behind,* it will *not* be an event to be witnessed only by His faithful friends. The whole world will have ringside seats!

And wouldn't you know it. The mighty Apocalypse at the end of the Bible agrees with Jesus' declaration: "Look! He is coming with the clouds; *every eye* will see him."[8]

Could it be any clearer? Yet our "Left Behind" friends will quickly shift the paradigm by suggesting that all these explosive and spectacular word pictures of Christ's second advent actually are a description of His "third" coming, which they call His "glorious appearing." He comes secretly at the beginning of the seven-year tribulation—and then comes gloriously and visibly the "third" time at the end of the tribulation.

But unfortunately for that "Left Behind" theory, the third reason in Matthew 24 powerfully refutes any such possibility!

Reason #3 as to why Matthew 24 does not support the "secret rapture" theory—Jesus describes the fate of those who are left behind.

And there can be no "secret rapture" with this fate! "Then two will be in the field; one will be taken and one will be left. Two women will be grinding meal together; one will be taken and one will be left."[9]

Yes, but doesn't that mean that some will be "left behind" as the novels and movie teach? Not at all. And the reason we can be so certain is found in the very obvious clue Jesus offers just before He gives this somber "one is taken; one is left" description:

> For as in those days before the flood they were eating and drinking, marrying and giving in marriage, until the day Noah entered the ark, and they knew nothing until the flood came and swept them all away, so too will be the coming of the Son of Man. Then two will be in the field; one will be taken and one will be left.[10]

Look—Jesus is saying—when I return to earth again, it will be just like it was at the flood. Life in its normal routines will be going on—people will be eating and drinking and marrying. Then suddenly I will appear. And it will be as it was with Noah—some will be taken, and some will be left—some of them out in the field, some of them at the mill, some even in bed. Just as it was in the flood, I will suddenly appear and "take" some of them.

In fact, the Greek word for "taken" here in Matthew 24 ("one will be taken") is the same Greek word Jesus speaks in the Upper Room in John 14: "I will come again and will *take* you to myself, so that where I am, there you may be also."[11] So, what Jesus is declaring in Matthew 24 is—yes, yes, when I come again I will *take* My friends to be with Me.

But now comes the critical truth that "Left Behind" left behind. Please note very carefully what happens to those who are left behind in the story Jesus is telling. It is incontrovertibly clear. Jesus plainly declares here in Matthew 24 that the ones who are left behind are swept away in destruction. *Just as in the flood!*[12] (The Greek word for "flood" here is *kataklysmos,* from whence comes our word "cataclysm"—which is exactly what the flood was and what the second coming will be!)

Left Behind—But Not Left Alive

Note it carefully: *Those who are left behind are not left to go on—for they are not left alive.*

And that is precisely why there cannot be a "third" coming of Jesus after a "secret" second coming. For the very passage in Matthew 24 that our "Left Behind" friends use to describe Jesus' secret coming plainly reveals that there would not be any inhabitants left to come back to, since those who are left are not left alive, but are swept away in destruction, "as it was in the days of Noah."

Remember the story of Sodom and Gomorrah? In Luke's parallel account of this passage in Matthew, Jesus adds that catastrophe to the flood narrative in order to make His point even more strongly!

> Likewise, just as it was in the days of Lot: they were eating and drinking, buying and selling, planting and building, but on the day that Lot left Sodom, it rained fire and sulfur from heaven and destroyed all of them; it will be like that on the day that the Son of Man is revealed.[13]

Notice the sequence. Lot was taken out of the city to safety— and what happened to those who were left behind? Just as in the flood, they were swept away by the supernatural cataclysm.

And then, just in case we might have missed His point, Jesus somberly adds: "Remember Lot's wife"—the woman who is remembered in history for being "left behind." And what was her fate? She was destroyed.

Anyway you wish to read the gospel record, Jesus' warning is somber and clear—*those who are left behind are not left to go on, for they are not left alive.*

There they are—three compelling reasons why Matthew is incontrovertibly clear: There is no secret coming of Christ ever, ever, ever!

#1—If anyone tells you so, he is not telling you the truth; don't believe him, because it will be gloriously spectacular.

#2—The second coming of Christ will be witnessed by the entire world.

#3—Those who are "left behind" are not left alive—they are swept away in the cataclysmic destruction at the end of the world.

But you say, "Wait a minute, Dwight—is the 'secret rapture' theory based solely on Matthew 24:36-42?" Actually, there are two other texts that those who believe in the "secret rapture" theory embrace in defense of their theory.

In both the "Left Behind" book and the movie, the heroes of the story who missed out on Christ's secret coming and were consequently "left behind" rummage around the neighborhood church and discover a video. It was recorded by the pastor of the congregation sometime before the pastor himself was raptured. He apparently knew that the rapture was coming. And again, I want to say this charitably—how he knew I do not know, given the paucity of any credible biblical evidence supporting the "secret rapture" theory.

But because the books are novels, the pastor can know anything he wants. So he records a message for those of his parishioners who, he knows, will be "left behind." In that recorded video message of the now-raptured pastor, these words of 1 Corinthians 15 are entered into the fictitious plot.

> Listen, I will tell you a mystery! We will not all die, but we will all be changed, in a moment, in the twinkling of an eye, at the last trumpet. For the trumpet will sound, and the dead will be raised imperishable, and we will be changed. For this perishable body must put on imperishability, and this mortal body must put on immortality.[14]

Does 1 Corinthians 15:51-53 support a secret rapture return of

Christ? Even a repeated reading of this passage yields not a solitary hint of a secret coming. Paul is simply but powerfully describing how Jesus' promise to "take you to myself" will transpire: The dead will be raised to immortal life, and the living will be clothed with immortality and will go home with Jesus. That's it—with nary a word about a secret rapture coming.

That leaves one other text the advocates of this theory like to quote:

> For the Lord himself, with a cry of command, with the archangel's call and with the sound of God's trumpet, will descend from heaven, and the dead in Christ will rise first. Then we who are alive, who are left, will be caught up in the clouds together with them to meet the Lord in the air; and so will be with the Lord forever. Therefore encourage one another with these words.[15]

A Convincingly Un-Secret Rapture!

Is the secret rapture there? Actually, it is from this text in its ancient Latin translation that the word "rapture" (from the Latin *rapio,* for "caught up") was originally derived. But "rapture" is simply that—a catching upward or a carrying away. Does rapture mean secret? Quite to the contrary, what we witness here in Paul's description of Jesus' second advent is a noisy and boisterous, explosive resurrection event that includes a trumpet blast, a shout, and a cry! And again, not even a single hint of a secret coming.

I repeat with all sincerity and conviction: There is not a shred of credible biblical evidence to support the theory that millions of readers and viewers the world over are being exposed to through "Left Behind." Much to the contrary, the Bible is replete from cover to cover with the dramatic description of what it will be like when Christ returns to this earth as King of kings and Lord of lords!

In fact, here they are: five very "un-secret" biblical descriptions of how Jesus will return soon to this earth:

1. With angels.

Remember Jesus' description of the angels accompanying Him in His return to earth at His second coming—"And he [the Son of Man] will send out his angels with a loud trumpet call, and they will gather his elect from the four winds, from one end of heaven to the other"?[16]

Do you remember the net effect of a single angel who descended from heaven at Jesus' glorious resurrection? According to Matthew's record, "for fear of him the guards shook and became like dead men."[17] If those burly Roman guards fell as dead men before just a single angel from heaven, can you imagine the net effect on earth when the entire horizon and the sky above it will be filled with these glorious beings who have been our unseen guardians all our lives! IMAX at $10^{1,000,000}$—ten to the millionth! Nobody will sleep through the second coming of Christ!

2. With the trumpet of God.

Both Jesus and Paul describe the trumpet of God blasting its silver notes at the second coming.[18] In fact, Paul embeds his reference to the trumpet in the very heart of one of the three key texts that rapture supporters use in an attempt to prove their theory.[19] Want to see what the net effect of one such trumpet blast was once upon a time? Remember when God came down to the summit of Mt. Sinai to give His eternal law in the Ten Commandments? "On the morning of the third day there was thunder and lightning, as well as a thick cloud on the mountain, and a blast of a trumpet so loud that all the people who were in the camp trembled."[20]

One Sabbath during our university worship service I invited one of the students to blow (blast, really!) his trumpet as loud as he could. I promise you—nobody was sleeping after that! If all Israel trembled with a trumpet blasting from atop a mountain, can you imagine the net effect when the trumpet sounds above all the earth!

Nobody will sleep through the second coming of Christ!

3. With power and great glory.

Those are Jesus' own words describing His return: "with power and great glory."[21] The Greek word for great is *mega*—which means the second advent will be a "mega" glory and power moment!

Nobody will sleep through the second coming of Christ!

4. With lightning and fire.

Mt. Sinai explodes with lightning and fire when God comes down in that spectacular appearing. What do you think the moment will be like when the entire horizon is set ablaze at Christ's return![22]

Here's how Peter describes the conflagration:

> The day of the Lord will come like a thief, and then the heavens will pass away with a loud noise, and the elements will be dissolved with fire, and the earth and everything that is done on it will be disclosed.[23]

The Unexpected Thief

Not a very secret sort of event, is it? Ah, but, you retort, doesn't Peter clearly describe Jesus' second coming as "a thief"? And of course, all thieves come secretly, don't they? Yes, that is true. But to understand what the Bible's "thief in the night" metaphor means, we need to carefully read the text again, this time to examine the context: "The day of the Lord will come like a thief, and then the heavens will pass away with a loud noise, and the elements will be dissolved with fire, and the earth and everything that is done on it will be disclosed." Clearly Peter is *not* describing a secret coming. There's too much IMAX surround-sound imagery in his words.

Instead, whenever the Scriptures use the "thief" metaphor, they are describing "unexpected" rather than "secret." Jesus Himself makes that point clearly at the end of His teaching on the second coming in Matthew 24: "Understand this: if the owner of the house had known in what part of the night the thief was coming, he would have stayed awake and would not have let his house be broken into."[24] Jesus likens His coming to a thief—not to illustrate its secrecy, but rather its *unexpectedness!*

Peter exclaims that the skies will explode with a loud noise when He comes as a thief! No secret here.

Nobody will sleep through the second coming of Christ!

5. With an earthquake.

When northwest India was stricken early in 2001 with a devasting killer quake that left 30,000 dead, no one who survived it could ever have described it as a secret event! The Apocalypse describes the earthquake that will accompany the return of Christ: "And there came flashes of lightning, rumblings, peals of thunder, and a violent earthquake, such as had not occurred since people were upon the earth, so violent was that earthquake."[25]

It is beyond our fathoming to wonder what this end-time earthquake will be like!

But one thing's for certain: Nobody will sleep through the second coming of Christ!

There they are—five very "un-secret" descriptions of the second advent. Mark it well—there will be nobody alive who will miss out on the most spectacular theophany (the "showing" of God) in the history of this world! "Aw, shucks—I slept through it—I wish someone had awakened me." There will be no human alive who misses the second coming of Jesus.

In fact—and this is a somber prediction—Revelation declares there will be many who will see Him coming and will beg to be hidden from His face.[26] Think about it. If the second coming of Christ were a secret witnessed only by the saved, why are the lost crying to be hidden from His majestic face?

No Second Chances

OK, OK, you've made your point—you may be saying by now—but so what, who cares, what difference does it make whether Jesus comes secretly or not? My friend, it will make all the difference in the world. Because you see, the most urgent truth of all that "Left Behind" has left behind is that *there is no second chance.*

The "Left Behind" books are riddled with a potentially fatal "second chance" teaching. I have kept a list in the covers of each book. Listen, for example, to the dangerous admonition the now "raptured" pastor gives on the video tape he prerecorded for those "left behind":

> It doesn't make any difference, at this point, why you're still on earth. You may have been too selfish or prideful or busy, or perhaps you simply didn't take the time to examine the claims of Christ for yourself. *The point now is, you have another chance.* Don't miss it.[27]

But, you ask, what's so dangerous about that bit of pastoral admonition? So you wake up and realize that you've got to reform your life! What could possibly be wrong with that?

But that's just it: There *IS* no chance to reform after the second coming of Christ! Thank God there are numerous "second chances" throughout this life. *But when Jesus returns, it's over!* After Jesus Christ returns to earth, you and I will have absolutely zero chances to change our lives and reform our ways. *There is NO second chance.*

Seven Years to Party Hearty

The "Left Behind" books and movie and the "secret rapture" theory all make you think that if perchance you miss getting raptured, at least you've got seven years to get your spiritual act together before Christ comes the "third" time.

So what do you suppose—human nature being what it is anywhere on earth—many of us would be tempted to do with that kind of proposition? You guessed it! "I'm going to 'party on, dude,' until the secret rapture—and then, when my pastor and the good members of my congregation mysteriously disappear, I'll know I've got seven more years to really get ready this time around!"

But for a moment, let's pretend that the "secret rapture" theory is true. Let me ask you: What would God gain from such a theory or truth? The answer: Absolutely nothing! Because what good is a foxhole friend!

When I was a boy and my mother or my father decided that I had broken the law of the home one too many times, it was then time for corporal punishment. And as they marched me down the hallway to the bedroom where I knew a certain belt was hanging, how many times on the frantic way to that strap did I experience a glorious and sudden conversion! And oh, how I shouted all the way to the bedroom, "I'll never do it again, Mommy and Daddy— I promise you with all my heart—I'll be the best boy you've ever had" (which in fact I was until my kid brother Greg came along)! Miraculous (and repeated) conversions aside, was there really any change in me?

What good is a foxhole friend, who all his or her life here on earth rejects God and has no stomach or heart or time for the Eternal, but who watches the calendar after the secret rapture and quickly reforms just in time to make the seven-year cutoff? God will win not a single genuine new friend in such a scenario.

Remember the Flood—and Sodom and Gomorrah

Which is precisely why there was no second chance after the flood, and there was no second chance after the destruction of Sodom and Gomorrah. Everybody had already made up his or her mind, and their fates were sealed by their own individual and personal choices. At that point God's mercy bowed to His justice— and the floods came to the antediluvians, and the fires came to Sodom and swept away all those left behind. Because there comes a point after which God declares, Enough is enough! "He who is unjust, let him be unjust still; she who is filthy, let her be filthy still; he who is righteous, let him be righteous still; and she that is holy, let her be holy still."[28]

Oh, it is true, Peter declares that "[God is] not willing that any should perish but that all should come to repentance."[29] Which is why He pleads so earnestly *today!* And yes, God will forgive you and me "seventy times seven" in this life—which calculates to 490 (or 489 second chances)![30] But once Jesus returns, it's over!

The Bible Isn't a Novel

"Left Behind" tries so hard to make it look as if it works, in making it appear that when God gives a second chance hundreds and thousands step forward and are converted. And when you're writing a novel, you can make it turn out anyway you wish. But when you're telling the truth, you must abide by the Word of Truth. And the Bible is absolutely clear. The second coming of Jesus and the final judgment are simultaneous, after which there are no more chances at all.

These words in Hebrews 9:27, 28 couldn't be any clearer—"And just as it is appointed for mortals to die once, and after that the judgment, so Christ, having been offered once to bear the sins of many, will appear a second time, not to deal with sin, but to save those who are eagerly waiting for him." How could the authors of "Left Behind" have missed this critical text? Clearly, once Christ returns the "second time," there is no more dealing with sin. The second coming of Christ will have the identical effect as death in bringing to an end the record of that human life. "And after that the judgment," in which every human choice is locked in for eternity: "He who is unjust, let him be unjust still; she who is filthy, let her be filthy still; he who is righteous, let him be righteous still; and she that is holy, let her be holy still."[31]

Which is why in the very next verse of Revelation 22, Christ declares: "See, I am coming soon; my reward is with me to repay according to everyone's work."[32] When Jesus comes again, He returns with the decisions of and for the entire human race already determined. There is no seven-year second chance! And if you're banking on one, you'll be lost.

Which is exactly why the bridegroom (in Jesus' parable) says what he says to the five foolish virgins who are pounding on the door and begging entrance. They weren't ready when He came the first time, and now they plead for a second chance. But sadly the Bridegroom declares to the five: "I can't let you in, for I do not know you."[33] Why doesn't God open the door? Because He wouldn't win a friend or change a heart even if He did!

Which is why God cries out to all of us who are living at the end of time, "*Today*, if you hear [My] voice, do not harden your hearts." "For behold, *now* is the acceptable time; behold, *now* is the day of salvation!"[34]

Which is why *now* is the very best time for a second chance with our Forever Friend. For *now* is the only time we have left.

"Even so, come, Lord Jesus."

Notes

[1]Tim Lahaye and Jerry B. Jenkins, *Left Behind*, pp. 15, 16.

[2]Matthew 24:36-42.

[3]Luke 17:34.

[4]Matthew 24:23-26, emphasis supplied.

[5]Matthew 24:27.

[6]Matthew 24:30, 31.

[7]Matthew 24:30, emphasis supplied.

[8]Revelation 1:7, emphasis supplied.

[9]Matthew 24:40, 41.

[10]Matthew 24:37-39.

[11]John 14:3.

[12]The KJV and the NKJV translation of Matthew 24:39—"the flood came and *took* them all away"—is confusing, because both translations use derivatives of the same English word *take* to translate two entirely different Greek words. In describing the destroying flood in verse 39, the Greek word (*airo*) signifies being "swept away" in destruction—hence the NRSV translation "the flood came and swept them all away." However, Jesus'

description of "one will be taken and one will be left" in verses 40 and 41 uses the more personal Greek for "receive to one's self" (*paralambano*)—as already noted, the same word Jesus used in the Upper Room in John 14:3.

[13]Luke 17:28-30.

[14]1 Corinthians 15:51-53.

[15]1 Thessalonians 4:16-18.

[16]Matthew 24:31.

[17]Matthew 28:4.

[18]Matthew 24:31; 1 Thessalonians 4:16

[19]1 Thessalonians 4:16-17.

[20]Exodus 19:16. See also 1 Thessalonians 4:16 and Matthew 24:31.

[21]Matthew 24:31.

[22]Exodus 19:16; Matthew 24:27.

[23]2 Peter 3:10.

[24]Matthew 24:43.

[25]Revelation 16:18.

[26]See Revelation 6:15-17.

[27]*Left Behind,* p. 214, emphasis supplied.

[28]Revelation 22:11, adapted.

[29]2 Peter 3:9, NKJV.

[30]See Matthew 18:22.

[31]See Revelation 22:11, adapted.

[32]Revelation 22:12.

[33]See Matthew 25:12.

[34]See Hebrews 3:15 and 2 Corinthians 6:2, emphasis supplied.

The Greatest Truth of All

TWO YOUNG GIRLS, about seven years of age, were awaiting surgery in the Hasbro Children's Hospital in Providence, Rhode Island, on Christmas Eve, 2000. One was waiting to have her tonsils removed; the other to have reconstructive eye surgery. In time the orderly arrived for one of the girls and wheeled her off to the waiting surgical amphitheater.

The tonsillectomy went smoothly and was completed in twenty minutes. The young patient was wheeled back out, and the orderly headed off to prepare the second girl for her eye surgery. Only then did hospital workers discover that they had just removed the tonsils and adenoids from the wrong girl! She wasn't supposed to be going home with a sore throat—she was supposed to have bandages on her eye. According to the Associated Press report, hospital officials said two workers had failed to check an identification bracelet and had subsequently been disciplined.

Why make such a big deal over such a small detail? The answer is obvious. Failing to check proper identification can be a very costly error!

Which is exactly what has happened in "Left Behind." Someone neglected to check for the proper identification, and as a consequence millions of sincere Bible students have been led to make a very costly mistake. And in that terrible mistake the greatest truth of all has been left behind!

The Stunning Origin of the Secret Rapture

Ever wonder where these runaway best-selling books and video came up with their "seven more years" between the secret coming of Christ and His eventual "glorious appearing," as they call His "third" coming? The answer is simple. There's been a terrible misunderstanding about a single verse in Daniel: "Then he shall confirm a covenant with many for one week; but in the middle of the week he shall bring an end to sacrifice and offering."[1]

But it is a stunning surprise to most evangelical Christians to discover that this "seven year tribulation" they were taught did not come from the Bible at all—it came from Rome! How did that come to be? Let's share a sixty-second flight through history to find the answer. Hold onto your seat—it's a fascinating discovery!

In 1590 a bearded Spanish priest named Francisco Ribera (1537-1591), a Jesuit scholar, completed a brand new commentary on the book of Revelation. It was the culmination of years of writing. Why a commentary on the Apocalypse? Because Rome desperately needed a new method of Bible prophetic interpretation to turn back the withering challenge of the Protestant Reformation. For the previous seventy years, Martin Luther, John Calvin and a host of Reformers—and before them John Wycliffe and John Hus, among others—had concluded on the basis of careful study of Bible prophecy that the Roman Church was the Antichrist power prophesied ages earlier in Daniel and Revelation.

And the more the Reformers thundered their prophetic discovery, the more difficult (you can certainly understand this) and precarious became Rome's position and perception in the public domain. So Rome convened the famed Council of Trent (mid-1500s) in search of new methodologies to turn aside the debilitating challenges of these Protestant Reformers. Which is what led Francisco Ribera to publish his commentary on Revelation in 1590.

Ribera devised a new method of Bible interpretation called "futurism," which (just as it sounds) is all about the future. What the Spanish priest did was to take all of Revelation's prophecies (except the earliest chapters) and apply them to the end-time rather than to the history of the Church. Included in his relegating to the future were the prophecies about the Antichrist, who would appear, Ribera calculated, during the last seven years of earth's history.

It really was a very neat and nifty prophetic paradigm shift. Heretofore, Bible scholars had observed a grand sweep of Christian history outlined in the apocalyptic prophecies. But now with the wave of his quill, Ribera and subsequent Roman scholars shifted and shoved, as it were, all major prophetic fulfillment into the distant future just before the end of the world. Thus they were now able to respond to the Protestant challenge "The Antichrist is here now!" by retorting, "You are wrong—we are not the Antichrist—for through careful examination we have determined that the Antichrist appears at the end of time—and as an evil man he will rule the world for three and a half years of earth's final seven years—it all happens in the future!"

Thus it was that Rome was able to avert and blunt future charges of being the prophesied Antichrist of Daniel and Revelation.

Futurism and Dispensationalism

But what is even more astounding and incredible is that the very weapon Rome used against Protestantism would be embraced within three centuries by the Protestants themselves! In less than 300 years, futurism would find a home among fundamentalist Christians.

Thanks to an Irish Anglican lawyer turned preacher named John Nelson Darby (1800-1882). Darby became the creative genius behind the Protestant equivalent of Rome's futurism—another new method of Bible and prophetic interpretation called *dispensationalism.* Only Darby added a creative twist to Ribera's method. For Darby was the one who devised the "secret rapture" concept and had Jesus return to earth secretly for His true followers. With them whisked away from the earth, Darby concluded, the Antichrist (an evil man, most likely a European) would quickly usurp world control, making a covenant with Israel and rebuilding their temple. But then, according to Darby's interpretation, dramatically in the middle of his seven-year rule, the Antichrist would abolish all sacrifices in that rebuilt temple, thus plunging the world into the utter chaos of "the great tribulation." After which Christ would return visibly at the end of the seven years to destroy the Antichrist and set up His millennial Kingdom.

A follower of John Darby named Cyrus Scofield came along and wrote this new theory into Bible notes, that have resulted in the most popular Bible sold today—*The Scofield Reference Bible,* the textbook of dispensationlism.

And that, with variations on the theme, is where the "Left Behind" books and the "Left Behind" movie all got their inspiration. From a Jesuit priest and an Irish preacher.

But isn't that teaching, in fact, in the Bible, too? *No, it is not.*

For the next few pages, let me show you what *is* in the Bible. And then you decide.

The Greatest Truth

Let's go to the book of Daniel and the very same chapter and the very same prophecy that Ribera and Darby dissected. Daniel 9—what Isaac Newton called the "the foundation stone of the Christian religion," what has been described as the "crown jewel of the Old Testament," what we're calling "the greatest truth of all."

> In the first year of Darius the son of Ahasuerus, of the lineage of the Medes, who was made king over the realm of the Chaldeans— in the first year of his reign I, Daniel, understood by the books the

number of the years specified by the word of the Lord through Jeremiah the prophet, that He would accomplish seventy years in the desolations of Jerusalem.[2]

What Daniel essentially is telling us is: "One day while I was reading the writings of the prophet Jeremiah, it suddenly hit me that God promised to return my people the Jews from our exile here in Persia to our beloved homeland at the end of seventy years of exile! I quickly did the arithmetic and realized that from when I was taken captive in 605 B.C. until now in the first year of Darius, 538 B.C., nearly sixty-eight years have already gone by. Which means the seventy years are nearly up! But it doesn't appear to me that any deliverance for us is coming. Something's wrong! And so I, Daniel, set my face toward the Lord God."

"Then I set my face toward the Lord God to make request by prayer and supplications, with fasting, sackcloth, and ashes."[3]

A Prophet's Passionate Pleading

Jacques Doukhan, professor of Hebrew at the theological seminary at Andrews University, in his intriguing new book, *Secrets of Daniel,* notes that what commences here—one of the most moving prayers in all literature—is actually the seventh prayer in the book of Daniel and by far the longest. Heretofore, Daniel has never written the revered name of God in the Old Testament, YHWH. But suddenly in this passionate pleading of the prophet, the name of the Lord now appears seven times. Cloaking himself with the very clothing of death—ashes and sackcloth—and embracing the very act of death—cessation of all food consumption—Daniel, in true Hebrew penitence, bows down before his Lord and God and pours out the choking cadence of this moving intercession.

> And I prayed to the Lord my God, and made confession, and said, "O Lord, great and awesome God, who keeps His covenant and mercy with those who love Him, and with those who keep His commandments, *we* have sinned and committed iniquity, *we* have done wickedly and rebelled, even by departing from Your precepts

and Your judgments. Neither have *we* heeded Your servants the prophets, who spoke in Your name to our kings and our princes, to our fathers and all the people of the land."[4]

It is truly a moving prayer—this plea of penitence from Daniel. He is arguably the most righteous man whose life is recorded in the Old Testament. Yet from his lips over and over again is his inescapable identification with the sins of his people. Take the time sometime to read this soul-stirring passage slowly and in its entirety. Let your own heart be moved by Daniel's confession.

But for now let's read the last two lines of his prayer:

O my God, incline Your ear and hear; open Your eyes and see our desolations, and the city which is called by Your name; for we do not present our supplications before You because of our righteous deeds, but because of Your great mercies. O Lord, hear! O Lord, forgive! O Lord, listen and act! Do not delay for Your own sake, my God, for Your city and Your people are called by Your name.[5]

An Instant Reply

And wouldn't you know it! No sooner do you pour your heart out to God in penitent trust and earnest seeking—then in that instant an answer like a shaft of light plummets from the throne room to your prayer room!

Now while I was speaking, praying, and confessing my sin and the sin of my people Israel, and presenting my supplication before the LORD my God for the holy mountain of my God, yes, while I was speaking in prayer, the man Gabriel, whom I had seen in the vision at the beginning, being caused to fly swiftly, reached me about the time of the evening offering. And he informed me, and talked with me, and said, "O Daniel, I have now come forth to give you skill to understand. At the beginning of your supplications the command went out, and I have come to tell you, for you are greatly beloved; therefore consider the matter, and understand the vision."[6]

What is about to follow is truly the most spectacular of all Bible prophecies. Like a piece of academic doctoral research, the entire divine message is first summarized in its opening line as a prophetic thesis statement:

> Seventy weeks are determined for your people and for your holy city, to finish the transgression, to make an end of sins, to make reconciliation for iniquity, to bring in everlasting righteousness, to seal up vision and prophecy, and to anoint the Most Holy.[7]

Jacques Doukhan notes an intentional linkage between the seventy years noted in verse 2 here in Daniel 9 and the seventy weeks noted here in verse 24. Professor Doukhan observes that these two references to "seventy" form a "chiastic" relationship. The word "chiasm" is from the letter *chi* in the Greek alphabet that is written as: X. If we would draw a large X, the "seventy years" of verse 2 would be on top of the X (chaism) and the "seventy weeks" of verse 24 would be on the bottom of the X. But there's more. Because in the Hebrew, the "seventy weeks" is actually written "weeks seventy." That means the second phrase is a reversal of order in the first phrase:

Doukhan notes that Daniel's intentional chiasm is to assist the Hebrew reader in understanding that the "years" and "weeks" are parallel. That means the "seventy weeks" of this Daniel 9 prophecy are to be interpreted as "seventy weeks *of years*"—which is precisely how both the Septuagint and the Revised Standard Version have translated this line.[8]

Clearly then the familiar measuring stick for prophetic symbolic time in the ancient Scripture—"one day equals one year"—can be used in this prophecy.[9] In fact, Doukhan notes that "the day-year principle of interpretation is probably the most ancient and the most solid principle of the exegesis [interpretation] of our passage."[10] Using that equivalence—and many of the church Fathers (Jerome, Justin Martyr, Augustine, Luther, et al) used this measurement for prophetic time—the seventy weeks of years become 490 (70 x 7) days of years.

Gabriel is informing Daniel that even as his people were subjected to seventy years of exile, even so God was going to grant to them another probation of seven times seventy years. "Your people will have 490 years, Daniel, during which the Messiah Himself will come." It is a truly astounding prophecy! "Seventy weeks are determined for your people and for your holy city, to finish the transgression, to make an end of sins, to make reconciliation for iniquity, to bring in everlasting righteousness, to seal up vision and prophecy, and to anoint the Most Holy."[11]

But when will this final probationary period begin? Gabriel is quick with the answer. "Know therefore and understand, that from the going forth of the command to restore and build Jerusalem until Messiah the Prince, there shall be *seven weeks and sixty-two weeks;* the street shall be built again, and the wall, even in troublesome times."[12]

Do the Math

Do the arithmetic:[13] 7 weeks + 62 weeks = 69 weeks x 7 = 483 days/years. Which simply means that the Messiah Himself will come 483 years after the command to restore and build Jerusalem. (See the chart of the full 490-year prophecy on page 51.)

Fortunately for Bible students throughout the centuries, that date for the final command to restore and rebuild Jerusalem is one of the most verified and certified dates in all the Old Testament. Ezra 7 records the final royal command for the Jews to return to Jerusalem and restore it. It came in the fifth month of the seventh year of Artaxerxes, which fell in the late summer or early autumn of 457 B.C. So if we add 483 years to 457 B.C. we arrive at A.D. 27. (You may have done the quick arithmetic by subtracting 483 from 457, but you got 26 instead—which is correct—except that whenever you cross from B.C. to A.D., you always need to add a year, since there was no year zero—i.e., nobody ever had to fill out an application form with the answer, "I was born in the year 0"!)

But what happened in A.D. 27? Does that date have any significance with the prophesied coming of the Messiah?

Read Luke 3:1—"Now in the fifteenth year of the reign of Tiberius Caesar, Pontius Pilate being governor of Judea, Herod being tetrarch of Galilee, his brother Philip tetrarch of Iturea and the region of Trachonitis, and Lysanias tetrarch of Abilene." Not exactly spellbinding drama, to be sure. But Luke is intentionally linking a particular event to an historical date, when he references the year of Caesar. By Jewish reckoning the fifteenth year of Tiberius Caeser's reign was in fact the fall of A.D. 27.

A Perfect Fit

And what happened at that time? Luke goes on in verses 21 and 22: "When all the people were baptized, it came to pass that Jesus also was baptized; and while He prayed, the heaven was opened. And the Holy Spirit descended in bodily form like a dove upon Him, and a voice came from heaven which said, 'You are My beloved Son; in You I am well pleased.'"

Clearly, Jesus was baptized in A.D. 27. Did you know that this is the only event in the entire life of Jesus that the Gospel record carefully correlates with a historical date? Not even His birth is dated! Only His baptism. In fact two of the gospels—Mark and John—skip His birth story completely and go immediately to His baptism!

What's so significant about Christ's baptism? The Holy Spirit, Luke notes, descended upon Jesus like a dove. And what did that signify? Read Acts 10:38—"God anointed Jesus of Nazareth with the Holy Spirit and with power, who went about doing good and healing all who were oppressed by the devil, for God was with Him." That is, Jesus was anointed by the Holy Spirit for His ministry as the Messiah there at His baptism in A.D. 27. In fact both the Hebrew *(Mashîach)* and Greek *(Christos)* words for "Messiah" mean "Anointed One." Which is precisely what Gabriel prophesied would happen! A.D. 27—it's a perfect fit!

Which now explains Jesus' mysterious proclamation after His baptism: "Now after John was put in prison, Jesus came to Galilee, preaching the gospel of the kingdom of God, and saying, 'The time is fulfilled, and the kingdom of God is at hand. Repent, and believe in the gospel.'"[14]

Prophetic Proof

Did you catch that? Following His baptism, Christ went about proclaiming, "The time is fulfilled." What time? The great time prophecy of Daniel 9, of course! No wonder Isaac Newton exclaimed that this was the foundation stone of the Christian religion! Mark it well: *This prophecy, given more than 530 years before Jesus was even born, provides incontrovertible proof that Jesus was the promised and predicted Messiah.* No other individual in all of human history could have fulfilled this divine prophecy made more than 530 years in advance!

But does the rest of this amazing prophecy fit? "And after the sixty-two weeks Messiah shall be cut off, but not for Himself; and the people of the prince who is to come shall destroy the city and the sanctuary. The end of it shall be with a flood, and till the end of the war desolations are determined. Then he shall confirm a covenant with many for one week; but in the middle of the week he shall bring an end to sacrifice and offering. And on the wing of abominations shall be one who makes desolate, even until the consummation, which is determined, is poured out on the desolate."[15]

Note carefully that we are dealing with the final week, the seventieth week, or the final seven years of this 490-year probationary period for Israel, the seven years from A.D. 27 to A.D. 34. During this crucial seven-year span, the Messiah would be "cut off," as verse 26 indicates. And, according to Gabriel, in the middle of the week (the middle or half of 7 = 3-1/2) He would bring an end to sacrifices as verse 27 states.

What is going on here?

Bible scholars are united in their consensus that the public ministry of Jesus covered a period of three and a half years. In fact, you can count in the gospel records four Passovers that Christ celebrated, thus confirming His three-and-a-half-year ministry.

Simple arithmetic tells us that if you add those three and a half years to the beginning date of Jesus' ministry at His baptismal anointing as Messiah in the Fall of A.D. 27, you will arrive at the Spring of A.D. 31 as the terminus date for the end of His public ministry. And, of course, the whole world knows that His end was brought about by His crucifixion and death, thus dating His crucifixion in the Spring of A.D. 31. Which is precisely when, more than 500 years earlier, Gabriel had predicted the Messiah would be cut off and bring sacrifices to an end!

A Bright and Shining Truth

Look what happened when Jesus died! "And Jesus cried out again with a loud voice, and yielded up His spirit. Then, behold, the veil of the temple was torn in two from top to bottom; and the earth quaked, and the rocks were split."[16]

Why was the veil mysteriously rent from top to bottom by unseen hands? Because there was no more need for sacrificial lambs. God Himself had become the sacrificial lamb in Christ. The old was forever gone—for the new had come!

Why, on the very night before He was crucified, Jesus celebrated the Last Supper with His disciples, and notice how He used the very words of Daniel 9 about that table: "And as they were eating, Jesus took bread, blessed and broke it, and gave it to the disciples and said, 'Take, eat; this is My body.' Then He took the cup, and gave thanks, and gave it to them, saying, 'Drink from it, all of you. For this is My blood of the new covenant, which is shed for many for the remission of sins.'"[17]

"This is My blood *for the new covenant.*" The old has passed away—and something new has come. Gabriel declared in Daniel 9:27 that the Messiah would "confirm a covenant with many" during the last week of that 490-year prophecy. And He did!

The bright and shining truth of Daniel 9 is that Jesus Christ is precisely who the Scriptures declare Him to be—the Messiah and Savior of the human race!

He was anointed in baptism at the hour the prophetic clock struck. He was crucified as the Lamb of God at the hour the prophetic clock struck. He came, He died, He rose again—just as the ancient scriptures predicted. There can be no other Saviour—for there is no other Messiah. Only God could have written that history more than five centuries in advance. And only God could have foretold "the greatest truth of all."

Clever—But Wrong

Which is why I solemnly must conclude that Ribera and Darby and Scofield and "Left Behind" have made a fatal mistake in cutting Christ out of the prophecy of Daniel 9 and substituting the Antichrist instead. What terrible logic would allow for such a switch! The only way Ribera's futurism and Darby's dispensationalism can concoct a "seven-year tribulation" at the end of the world is to surgically excise the seventieth week of Daniel 9 and shove it 2,000 years later to the end of time.

It is a clever way to get seven years at the end, but it is wrong. For logic requires that the 70th week must follow the 69th week—or it can't be called the 70th week, now can it?

It is a clever way to get seven years at the end, but it is wrong! For there is not a single hint of a 2,000-year gap anywhere in the prophecy.

It is a clever way to get seven years at the end, but it is wrong! For Daniel 9:27 says absolutely nothing about a seven-year period of tribulation or even less than nothing about any Antichrist at all.

It is a clever way to get seven years and the Antichrist at the end, but it is wrong! For it destroys "the greatest truth of all!"

By removing the only time prophecy in all of Scripture that identifies Jesus of Nazareth as the divine Messiah and Saviour of the world, it carves Jesus out of the heart of Daniel. And I can think of only one being in the universe who would desire Christ cut out of so resplendent and convincing a proof.

Sometimes Fiction IS Stranger Than Truth!

So which would you rather have? Seven years at the end? Or salvation at the cross? By cutting off the seventieth week of Daniel 9, "Left Behind" is left with no Saviour at all. Which means that in this case, the fiction is stranger than the truth!

We have shared very plainly and candidly in this chapter, I realize. And I want to be quick to testify that there are many sincere and devout Christians who subscribe to dispensationalism unwittingly and unknowingly. You may be among them. And I do not wish to condemn you—not at all. I only wish to warn you earnestly that you have built your house of prophecy upon the sand. But you and I both know that unless we build our house upon the Rock of Christ Jesus, when the final storm strikes we and our house will be lost in the end.

The truth is: the theory is wrong. There is no seven-year second chance. When Jesus returns, that's it. Which is why we *must* build on the Rock and Word of Christ now.

Remember the Christmas Eve identification mixup in surgery? A hasty mistake in failing to check the young girl's identification cost somebody his job. But identifying the Messiah of Daniel 9 as the Antichrist is a mistake more terrible that will cost more than a job. So much more. Because at stake is the greatest truth of all.

And that truth is the Messiah Himself. It's your choice.

"Even so, come, Lord Jesus."

Notes:

[1]Daniel 9:27. The Bible quotations in this chapter are all from the *New King James Version.*

[2]Daniel 9:1, 2.

[3]Daniel 9:3.

[4]Daniel 9:4-6, emphasis supplied.

[5]Daniel 9:18, 19.

[6]Daniel 9:20-23.

[7]Daniel 9:24.

[8]For a more detailed and technical explanation of this chaistic parallel in Daniel, see Jacques Doukhan, *Secrets of Daniel,* pp. 143, 144.

[9]See Ezekiel 4:6 and Numbers 14:34.

[10]Doukhan, p. 145.

[11]Daniel 9:24.

[12]Daniel 9:25, emphasis supplied.

[13]On page 51 is a prophetic graph, charting the expanse of this amazing prophecy.

[14]Mark 1:14, 15.

[15]Daniel 9:26, 27.

[16]Matthew 27:50, 51.

[17]Matthew 26:26-28.

The 490 years of Daniel 9

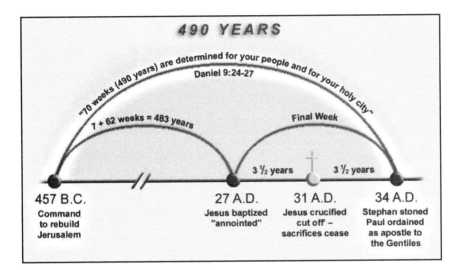

The Most Clarifying Truth of All

YOU CAN'T MISS IT: The "Left Behind" movie and the "Left Behind" books are *big* on Israel. The title block to the movie is minutes of stunning and sweeping photography of scenes from modern-day Jerusalem—the gilded dome of the Temple mount glinting in the noonday sun, the boisterous crowded alleyways below crammed with the cacophony of bazaars and market stalls and shops, the sacred Western Wall where the orthodox and the devout gather night and day to pray and weep before the remnants of their ancient temple foundation. And all the while the cameras are sweeping over the holy city, the theme music of "Left Behind" plays a haunting Hebrew melody through each Jerusalem scene.

Why is "Left Behind" so big on Israel? I'll let the authors of the best-selling books speak for themselves. Here is what Tim LaHaye and Jerry Jenkins have written in a companion book to the "Left Behind" series, *Are We Living in the End Times?*:

> Has it ever seemed strange to you that almost every night on the evening news the eyes of the world focus on a little country of five million in the Middle East? And only recently has China, a nation of 1.2 billion people, gained recognition on the international news airwaves. But seldom does Mexico City, one of the

largest population centers in the world, draw international atten-
tion. Singapore is similarly out of the news . . . . Those enormous
centers of world population regularly stay out of the news—but
when did a week last go by when Israel and Jerusalem did *not* fill
the world's headlines? Why this remarkable focus on a little coun-
try in the Middle East?[1]

Then LaHaye proceeds to answer his own question. Unfortunately the answer is half right and half wrong—which throws
us into quite a confusing conundrum indeed:

> The answer is simply that the Hebrew and Christian prophets
> had so much to say about Israel and Jerusalem in the end times
> . . . Jerusalem—mentioned in prophecy more than any other city
> on earth—will be a pain in the neck to the rest of the world, just as
> it seems to be today. . . . It is not the headquarters of any world
> government body or banking institution—yet it remains at the
> center of world attention.[2]

Israel in the Middle?

Because "Left Behind" is endeavoring to popularize a brand of
prophetic interpretation called dispensationalism (as we noted in
the previous chapter), it is vital for the movie and books to boldly
(and mistakenly, I might add, as we will discover in a moment)
place Israel in the middle of end-time events.

In fact, Tim LaHaye is so convinced he is right about Israel at
the end of time, that he makes this astounding claim:

> I call the regathering of five million Jews back to the Holy Land
> and their becoming a nation in our generation [in 1948] "the in-
> fallible sign" of the approach of the end times. . . . There are so
> many promises in the Scripture that God would eventually regather
> the children of Israel back into their land, that if none could be
> found in the twentieth century to be made into a nation, the Bible
> would have been revealed as a fraud.[3]

Question: But what if we discovered that in fact the Bible never
did prophesy that Israel would return as a political nation at the
end of time?

Answer: Then it wouldn't be the Bible that was the fraud, now would it?

We must explore what "Left Behind" left behind this time: the most clarifying truth of all. Because if you want to know the difference between what is truth and what is fraud, then you'd better know the truth about Israel.

Conditional Promises

A truth that begins with a single word: *Conditional.* What does the word *conditional* mean? That's fairly obvious—it has to do with certain "conditions" being met before anticipated results can follow.

When my parents used to come to me (and I imagine your parents did the same with you) to "bribe" me into being good (and of course, it really wasn't a bribe—we now call it a "motivational incentive"), they would say something like this: "All right, Dwight—*if* you will not pick on your brother Greg for a whole day, and *if* you will be kind to your little sister Kari all day long, *then* we will take you down to the village candy store and buy you your favorite sweets." Clearly, they were making a conditional promise to me. *If* you do thus and so, *then* you will receive this or that.

But of course, there were those times when they could make conditional warnings instead: "*If* you ever do that again, *then* [read my lips] we will warm a certain portion of your anatomy in order to heat up the truth in another portion of the same said anatomy . . . do you understand?" And oh boy, did I ever understand their conditional warnings! *If* you do thus and so, *then* you will receive this or that.

Now, I must be quick to interject that my parents' love for me was never conditional. They didn't say—"*If* you behave in this way, *then* we will love you as our son." I knew all through my boyhood days that Mom and Dad loved me no matter how I behaved or didn't behave, as the case may have been. So the issue was never their love for me.

Which, by the way, is the way it has been with God and His children from the very beginning. To Adam and Eve, God's love promised: "*If* you will trust Me and accept My word and stay away from this tree, *then* you may live in the Garden forever. But *if* you choose not to trust Me, and you disobey My command and eat from this tree, *then* you may not live in this Garden. And you will die." God's promises and God's warnings alike have always been conditional. But just like my parents' love, His love never has been and never will be conditional. "No matter how you behave, I will love you to the end."

Freedom to Choose

But that's just it—it is precisely because God's love is *unconditional* that His promises and warnings are *always conditional*. Divine love is too committed to human freedom to have it any other way: "Because I love you and am committed to your freedom to freely choose your path in life, I will not force you to choose My way. *If* you choose My way, *then* I promise you, you will discover the way of Life eternal. But *if* you prefer not to choose My way, *then* it is only fair I warn you that you will discover the way of Death—for when you separate from Me, you separate from Life itself."

Or as the apostle John so succinctly put it: "Whoever has the Son has life; whoever does not have the Son of God does not have life."[4] God's promise is clear, but the choice is ours.

I repeat: it is precisely because God's love is unconditional that His promises and warnings have always been conditional. He will always let us choose.

But you say, "OK, OK—you've made the point—but I thought we were talking about Israel—what in the world do conditional promises and conditional warnings have to do with Israel?" The answer is—conditional promises and conditional warnings have everything in the world to do with Israel. Which, unfortunately, "Left Behind" left behind.

So fasten your seat belt—and let's fly through some ancient history together.

The mighty exodus from Egypt is now history! The liberated slaves are on their way home—a brand-new home in Canaan. But at the foot of the rocky crag called Sinai, God gathers the children of Israel for a family council. And He summons their leader to the summit for the council agenda:

> Then Moses went up to God, and the Lord called to him from the mountain and said, "This is what you are to say to the house of Jacob and what you are to tell the people of Israel: 'You yourselves have seen what I did to Egypt, and how I carried you on eagles' wings and brought you to myself. Now *if* you obey me fully and keep my covenant, *then* out of all nations you will be my treasured possession. Although the whole earth is mine, you will be for me a kingdom of priests and a holy nation.' These are the words you are to speak to the Israelites."[5]

If—Then

There it is, the telltale *if—then* formula of a conditional promise—do you see it? "*If* you obey me . . . *then* you will be my treasured possession."

Unfortunately, the sad story of Israel is embarrassingly familiar, because it's the story of all of our lives—namely, just like us, Israel lived a roller coaster life with God—up one year and then down the next—over and over and over again!

I read the Pentateuch and the books of history through a few weeks ago, and how familiar the story:

> The people worshiped the Lord all the days of Joshua, and all the days of the elders who outlived Joshua, who had seen all the great work that the Lord had done for Israel. . . . [But] then the Israelites did what was evil in the sight of the Lord and worshiped the Baals. . . . [So] whenever they marched out, the hand of the Lord was against them to bring misfortune, as the Lord had warned

them and sworn to them; and they were in great distress. . . . [Then] the Lord raised up judges for them, the Lord was with the judge, and he delivered them from the hand of their enemies all the days of the judge; for the Lord would be moved to pity by their groaning because of those who persecuted and oppressed them. But whenever the judge died, they would relapse and behave worse than their ancestors."[6]

Promises and Warnings

This spiritual "manic-depressive" cycle continues throughout the ancient story. Because after the judges, they beg for a king, and promise God it will be better this time. And for a while it was. But soon it became a litany and history of good king, bad king, good king, bad king—up and down, up and down. Until finally, God throws up His hands, as it were, and in Jeremiah 7 makes a last impassioned plea with Israel before their exile. The classic *if—then* formula of conditional promises and warnings can't be missed here!

> Thus says the Lord of hosts, the God of Israel: "Amend your ways and your doings, and let me dwell with you in this place. Do not trust in these deceptive words: 'This is the temple of the Lord, the temple of the Lord, the temple of the Lord.'
>
> For *if* you truly amend your ways and your doings, *if* you truly act justly one with another, *if* you do not oppress the alien, the orphan, and the widow, or shed innocent blood in this place, and *if* you do not go after other gods to your own hurt, *then* I will dwell with you in this place, in the land that I gave of old to your ancestors forever and ever."[7]

Essentially, God is crying out: "I wanted you to have the land forever, *but* you will not get to live in this land much longer, *unless* you amend your ways and return to Me." Once again, it is the classic *if—then* formula of conditional promises and conditional warnings. And Jeremiah goes on to point out the classic *if—then* formula for conditional prophecy, too:

> If at any time I announce [God is speaking] that a nation or kingdom is to be uprooted, torn down and destroyed, and *if* that nation I warned repents of its evil, *then* I will relent and not inflict

on it the disaster I had planned. And if at another time I announce that a nation or kingdom is to be built up and planted, and *if* it does evil in my sight and does not obey me, *then* I will reconsider the good I had intended to do for it.[8]

Yes, you say, but that has to do with the other nations and not Israel itself. Oh really? Read the very next verse:

> Now therefore say to the people of Judah and those living in Jerusalem, "This is what the Lord says: Look! I am preparing a disaster for you and devising a plan against you. So turn from your evil ways, each one of you, and reform your ways and your actions."[9]

In other words, "You're on a fast track to destruction. But *if* you will amend your ways, *then* I will change My mind." God's promises and prophecies alike are conditional.

The classic proof of that is the story of Jonah and Nineveh. God comes to Jonah with simple instructions: "Go tell Nineveh, Jonah, that I'm going to nuke their wicked city in forty days!" Jonah obeys (after a slight detour through the belly of a whale) and marches into that wicked urban center and preaches the end of the world! And wonder of wonders—those pagan city dwellers with their very pagan king are moved to tears by the message of impending judgment—a revival breaks out—and God changes His mind! Forgives the entire city, and abandons His prophecy to vaporize them in forty days! (Much to Jonah's consternation, by the way, over his ruined reputation as a true prophet of God.)

Free to Say "No"

It is too bad and really quite sad that Israel and Jerusalem didn't respond to God as did their pagan antagonists—Nineveh and later Nebuchadnezzar. They left God no choice. He had been clear with them—His promises are conditional. So honoring their freedom to say No to Him, the heartbroken God of Jeremiah and Jonah allows His children to be led away into exile—letting them reap the inevitable consequences of their choice to live apart from their divine Protector and Friend and Guardian and Father.

But even then, the heart of divine Love refuses to let them go without another chance. And so while Daniel is pleading with God to fulfill His promise to return Israel to their homeland after those seventy years of exile, God honors His loyal friend's faith and discloses to Daniel the breathtaking prophecy of Daniel 9. Remember Gabriel's words: "Seventy weeks are decreed for your people and holy city."[10] That is: Listen to me carefully, Daniel— God has sent me with the message that your people Israel and your holy city Jerusalem have "seventy weeks of years" of probation left.

Probation Isn't Forever

Did your mother ever do that to you? Look you straight in the eye and announce: "You've got thirty seconds to make up your mind!" We learned it very early in life, didn't we? Whenever parents add a time limit to their conditional promise or warning, we knew beyond the shadow of a doubt that they were utterly serious about the matter! (When Mama says you have thirty seconds—it is both pointless and dangerous to ask for forty-five! Better to respond in fifteen!)

"Your people Israel have seventy weeks, Daniel. I am giving them 490 more years (the length of seventy prophetic weeks, as we learned in the last chapter)—one last probation to return to Me and stay with Me forever. But when the probation is up, that's it."

And true to His covenant and true to His loving form, when the probationary time period for the nation of Israel was nearing its end, God pulled out every stop He had left and in fulfillment of Daniel 9, He sent His Son the Messiah! "But when the fullness of time had come [according to Daniel 9's prophecy], God sent his Son, born of a woman, born under the law."[11]

And from the moment of His anointing by the Holy Spirit at His baptism (remember, *Messiah* means "the anointed one"), Jesus was immensely popular with the Jewish masses. He was *their* hero.

Wherever He went, they freely and openly cheered Him as the "Son of David" (a well-known Messianic title). For three and a half years the One who was adulated and adored as the Messiah moved about freely in their midst—teaching them and healing them and comforting them and leading them. No question, Jesus was their favorite Son.

But He was envied and hated by the ecclesiastical and political leadership of that land. And it cut Jesus to the very core of His being. Until finally at the end of His three and half years of Messianic ministry He could take it no longer. And twice He publicly burst into tears!

> As he approached Jerusalem and saw the city, he wept over it and said, "If you, even you, had only known on this day what would bring you peace—but now it is hidden from your eyes. The days will come upon you when your enemies will build an embankment against you and encircle you and hem you in on every side. They will dash you to the ground, you and the children within your walls. They will not leave one stone on another, because you did not recognize the time of God's coming to you.[12]

Tears for What Might Have Been

In words too somber to miss, Christ predicts that the ending to Daniel 9's seventieth week will come true for that generation—and He weeps over what might have been. The crowds adored him, but Jesus weeps for the capital and its rulers:

> O Jerusalem, Jerusalem, you who kill the prophets and stone those sent to you, how often I have longed to gather your children together, as a hen gathers her chicks under her wings, but you were not willing. Look, your house is left to you desolate. For I tell you, you will not see me again until you say, "Blessed is he who comes in the name of the Lord."[13]

The tears of the heartbroken Messiah, who knows that probation is about to end: "It is over for your House, O Israel. This temple will never again be strategic in the divine economy of salvation—never again. I leave it to you desolate. It is over."

Have you ever listened to a mother weeping over her son or her daughter who has rejected her maternal love? I have. And I can tell you it is a deep and terrible pain that erupts in those anguished and choking sobs of a mother whose heart is irreparably broken. I hope never to hear it again.

In Christ Jesus we are confronted with the anguish of unrequited divine love. God does not stop loving. Rather He has stopped being loved. And when God is spurned and turned away, what choice is there left for Him?

In answer Jesus tells a heartbreaking parable on the eve of His own death:

> Listen to another parable: There was a landowner who planted a vineyard. He put a wall around it, dug a winepress in it and built a watchtower. Then he rented the vineyard to some farmers and went away on a journey. When the harvest time approached, he sent his servants to the tenants to collect his fruit.
>
> The tenants seized his servants; they beat one, killed another, and stoned a third. Then he sent other servants to them, more than the first time, and the tenants treated them the same way. Last of all, he sent his son to them. "They will respect my son," he said.
>
> But when the tenants saw the son, they said to each other, "This is the heir. Come, let's kill him and take his inheritance." So they took him and threw him out of the vineyard and killed him.
>
> Therefore, when the owner of the vineyard comes, what will he do to those tenants?
>
> "He will bring those wretches to a wretched end," they replied, "and he will rent the vineyard to other tenants, who will give him his share of the crop at harvest time."
>
> Jesus said to them, "Have you never read in the Scriptures: 'The stone the builders rejected has become the capstone; the Lord has done this, and it is marvelous in our eyes'? Therefore I tell you that the kingdom of God will be taken away from you and given to a people who will produce its fruit."[14]

And most Christians have stopped the story right there, and concluded that Jesus was teaching that God rejected the Jews. And because of that skewed thinking, atrocities like the Holocaust have been perpetrated against the Jews throughout the history of Christianity. How sad!

A History of Heartache

Could a history of heartache been avoided had we only read the very next verses? A simple reading of them makes it utterly clear who it was who rejected Christ:

> When the chief priests and the Pharisees heard Jesus' parables, they knew he was talking about them. They looked for a way to arrest him, but they were afraid of the crowd because the people held that he was a prophet.[15]

Clearly the masses regarded Jesus as a prophet. It was not they, but the rulers, who rejected him. Note it carefully— Matthew 21 will not sanction either of two rampant errors being taught today:

Error #1—God has rejected the Jews.

The Apostle Paul is clear: "I ask, then, has God rejected his people? By no means! I myself am an Israelite, a descendant of Abraham, a member of the tribe of Benjamin. God has not rejected his people whom he foreknew."[16] God has not rejected His children. The Jews are not a rejected people today, any more than on the basis of Christianity's failure during the Dark Ages we ourselves are a rejected people today. The sins of our fathers are not held against us. Which, however, does not sanction error #2.

Error #2—Israel as a political nation still has a place in divine prophecy.

It does not. All those Old Testament prophecies that our dispensationalist friends are hoping and teaching will yet come literally true were *all conditional.* They have missed that critical point. "*If* as a nation, you stay with Me as your God, *then* I will stay with you as My nation. But *if* you reject Me as a nation, *then* I will then give the kingdom to another nation." Hence Jesus' mournful words: "Therefore I tell you, the kingdom of God will be taken away from you and given to a people [Greek—*ethnos*—'a nation'] that produces the fruit of the kingdom."[17]

And what new "nation" would that be? "But you are a chosen race, a royal priesthood, *a holy nation,* God's own people, in order that you may proclaim the mighty acts of him who called you out of darkness into his marvelous light. Once you were not a people, but now you are God's people; once you had not received mercy, but now you have received mercy."[18]

In a telling linkage with the Old Testament, Peter quotes the very words God spoke to Moses atop Mt. Sinai, when He declared that the children of Israel would become His people[19]—only now Peter applies that promise to a new "nation," a new "people." Then Peter hearkens back to the ancient prophet Hosea and again seizes a promise originally made to the nation of Israel and reapplies it to this new "people."[20]

And who is this new nation? Paul responds:

> As many of you as were baptized into Christ have clothed your-selves with Christ. There is no longer Jew or Greek, there is no longer slave or free, there is no longer male and female; for all of you are one in Christ Jesus. And if you belong to Christ, then you are Abraham's offspring, heirs according to the promise.[21]

Paul literally expresses it in the Greek—"you are Abraham's *sperma,*" which the King James translates "seed." That is a fairly direct lineage, wouldn't you say! You are the "sperm" of Abraham. We're not talking distant cousins here!

And if Abraham is your spiritual father, then what does that make you? Paul has the answer at the end of the same letter:

> May I never boast of anything except the cross of our Lord Jesus Christ, by which the world has been crucified to me, and I to the world. For neither circumcision nor uncircumcision is anything; but a new creation is everything! As for those who follow this rule— peace be upon them, and mercy, and upon *the Israel of God.*[22]

There it is—God has a new Israel! The new "Israel of God" are Jews and Greeks, slaves and free, males and females. A new community of faith that is but the continuation of God's dream from the very beginning. That He would have a people on earth loyal to Him above all else, a people passionately devoted to their Creator and Redeemer, even as He is passionately devoted to them. A people, "a holy nation," no longer bound by political borders or geographic boundaries. A people no longer a local theocracy, but now a global community. A people who encompass all the peoples of earth and who bring God's salvation to all the nations of the world.

A Rebuilt Temple in Jerusalem?

And what does this truth have to do with "Left Behind"? It's the truth that "Left Behind" left behind. You see, "Left Behind" desperately wants and needs a reactivated Israel and a rebuilt temple in Jerusalem as a part of its end-time strategy. But it is not God's end-time strategy.

Yes, it is possible that the temple may be rebuilt one day. But it will never be a part of God's plan. Why? Because of what Jesus told the woman at the well about the Messiah:

> Jesus said to her, "Woman, believe me, the hour is coming when you will worship the Father neither on this mountain [Mt. Gerazim in Samaria] nor in Jerusalem. . . . God is spirit, and those who worship him must worship in spirit and truth." The woman said to him, "I know that Messiah is coming" (who is called Christ). "When he comes, he will proclaim all things to us." Jesus said to her, "I am he, the one who is speaking to you."[23]

Notice carefully Jesus' declaration. Once the Messiah—the great I AM—comes, there will be no need for a geographical temple on earth. For the Messiah Himself will be the divine fulfillment of everything Israel's temple once stood for. Which is why when the Messiah cried out "It is finished!" as He died atop that Good Friday cross, the veil of Israel's Temple was rent in half from top to bottom.[24] Never again would the Jerusalem Temple be a strategic part of God's plan of salvation. When Christ died as the Lamb of God, the Temple sacrificial system was forever ended.

Hence the words of Jesus to the woman—"the hour is coming when you will worship the Father neither on this mountain nor in Jerusalem"—are compelling evidence that indeed God has *no* plans ever to rebuild any temple anywhere on earth, let alone Jerusalem.

That is why it is very unfortunate that "Left Behind" and dispensationalists are being utterly distracted by what is happening in Israel today. Tim LaHaye's exclamation at the beginning of this chapter that the return of the Jews to Israel is an "infallible sign" of the approaching end-times completely misses the truth about God's conditional promises and prophecies to ancient Israel. While it is true that the United States has been historically allied with Israel, and while it is possible that the temple in Jerusalem someday may be rebuilt, neither of those actions are acts of God—they are acts of government. And that is a very big difference.

Of course God loves the Jewish people. They are just as much His children as are the Arab people and the Christian people of the earth. But a careful examination of Holy Scripture reveals the very clarifying and compelling truth that God has burst all the ethnic and racial and geographical boundaries of old, and that today the new Israel of God are His forever friends in "every nation and tribe and language and people."[25]

But I must confess a deeper concern regarding this truth "Left Behind" has left behind. For I fear "Left Behind" is being distracted by political events in Israel for a very dangerous reason. The Antichrist even now is stealthfully on the move across the face of this earth. Evangelical distraction with Israel is blinding far too many from the greater danger that is about to sweep the world.

Now more than ever we must pray.

"Even so, come, Lord Jesus."

Notes:

[1] Tim LaHaye and Jerry B. Jenkins, *Are We Living in the End Times?*, p. 45.

[2] *Ibid.,* pp. 45, 46.

[3] *Ibid.,* pp. 47-49.

[4] 1 John 5:12.

[5] Exodus 19:3-6, NIV, emphasis supplied.

[6] Judges 2:7, 11, 15, 18, 19.

[7] Jeremiah 7:3-7, emphasis supplied.

[8] Jeremiah 18:7-10, NIV, emphasis supplied.

[9] Jeremiah 18:11, NIV.

[10] Daniel 9:24

[11] Galatians 4:4.

[12] Luke 19:41-44, NIV.

[13] Matthew 23:37-39, NIV.

[14] Matthew 21:33-43, NIV.

[15] Matthew 21:45, 46, NIV.

[16] Romans 11:1, 2.

[17] Matthew 21:43.

[18] 1 Peter 2:9, 10.

[19] Exodus 19:6.

[20] See Hosea 2:23.

[21] Galatians 3:27-29.

[22] Galatians 6:14-16, emphasis supplied.

[23] John 4:21, 24-26.

[24] See John 19:30 and Matthew 27:50, 51.

[25] See Revelation 14:6.

The Most Dangerous Truth of All

THE HEADLINE CAUGHT my eye: "What's gray and dances in Mexico?" Since I couldn't conjure up a sensible answer, I read on:

> Benny, a 9-year-old with a talent for the harmonica, sneaked into Mexico from Texas with the help of a $4,500 bribe. Sped along by a shadowy go-between and corrupt customs agents who made him "invisible," Benny got into his new country, found a job, changed his name and tried to live a decent life.[1]

Now, I'm really curious! Turns out they hid Benny inside a wooden box on the back of a flatbed truck. But apparently he was as quiet as a mouse (which is an inappropriate metaphor, given Benny's notorious skittishness around mice!), because he got into Mexico without detection. And the Mexicans are absolutely delighted (though Benny's clandestine flight across the border violated laws in both Mexico and the United States)—because at last the tables have been turned, and now it's an *American* who's been caught as an illegal alien in Mexico! Lawyers are trying to sort out the legal conundrum. But in the meantime, Benny keeps dancing. In a circus outside Mexico City. For Benny, you see, is a 9-year-old pachyderm—a lumbering gray Asian elephant!

Sometimes with a little bit of luck and enough blind eyes, you can steal an elephant out from under everybody's nose. It was a clever deception that has citizens south and north of the border chuckling.

Global Deception

But it is no laughing matter when we are confronted with the greatest spiritual deception ever perpetrated on earth. A colossal deception of global proportions defined by a single word: *Antichrist.* For millennia now, the flashing red light of apocalyptic warning about this deception has ominously pulsated from the heart of Holy Scripture. Yet out from under our very noses, something sacred has been stolen, something sinister has been substituted. Antichrist. The most dangerous truth of all.

A truth so dangerous it is absolutely no wonder or surprise to me that "Left Behind" would also leave this truth behind. It is simply too dangerous a truth. It cannot be shared publicly for long without exacting a fearful price—a price "Left Behind" was obviously not willing to pay.

Although, according to the *Wall Street Journal,* $17.5 million was spent to produce the "Left Behind" movie that has now been released to the public.[2] But alas for the producers and investors. The public response on the opening weekend of February 2, 2001, was both dismal and disappointing. Reportedly their goal had been to screen the "Left Behind" movie simultaneously in 3800 theaters nationally—but only 874 theaters agreed to premier it. And only $2.2 million revenue came in opening weekend to offset the $17.5 million price tag.[3]

But forget the dollars-and-cents price tag. Because at what price does *truth* get left behind? This much we can all agree upon: Truth is worth any price. And so it is imperative that we share here "the most dangerous truth of all," irrespective of the price it will exact. It is the truth about the Antichrist, a truth "Left Behind" left behind.

Please don't misunderstand me. "Left Behind" is very big on the Antichrist. It's just that it's wrong.

Let's watch a scene from the first novel in the series, also captured in the movie. The setting is in the United Nations building, an administrative boardroom somewhere deep inside the familiar New York City edifice. Gathered about the mahogany table are several leading ambassadors, two wealthy English financiers, some personal assistants, one journalist, and the newly elected Secretary General of the United Nations.

The Secretary General is a young, blond, blue-eyed Romanian named Nicolae Carpathia. Charismatic, smooth, controlling, but disarming, the Romanian politician has risen with breathtaking speed (according to the book) to a position of global leadership. Adored by the masses and adulated by the media, Nicolae Carpathia will become (though the reader and viewer do not know it yet) the dreaded Antichrist in "Left Behind."

Nicolae Carpathia begins to speak. Methodical but mesmerizing, he recounts to his invitees the necessary measures that have been taken to unite the world in the face of the recent global crisis—the simultaneous disappearances of millions of earth inhabitants (the secret rapture of "Left Behind"). And with an air of self-congratulations, he announces to the chamber:

> Gentlemen . . . and lady . . . this is an important moment. In a few minutes we will greet the press and introduce those of you who shall be entrusted to lead the new world order into a golden era. The global village has become united, and we face the greatest task and the greatest opportunity ever bestowed upon humankind.[4]

Concluding his penetrating monologue, young Nicolae quietly requests the security guard's sidearm, and with cool dispatch murders the two Englishmen who stand in his way, after which, through mind control (remember, this is fiction), he manipulates everyone in the room into believing that the two men killed themselves—everyone in the room except, of course, for Buck Williams, the "left behind" journalist lately become Christian believer. The stage is now set for the novels' protagonist and antagonist.

What are the "Left Behind" books and movie trying to tell us or teach us? The Antichrist is soon to come! Here is how Tim LaHaye puts it in his prophetic primer that is a companion book to the "Left Behind" series:

> Scripture indicates that there will be a great lie, announced with the help of the media and perpetrated by a self-styled world leader. . . . Let me warn you personally to beware of such a leader of humanity who may emerge from Europe. He will turn out to be a great deceiver who will step forward with signs and wonders that will be so impressive that many will believe he is of God. He will gain a great following among those who are left [behind], and many will believe he is a miracle worker.
>
> The deceiver will promise strength and peace and security, but the Bible says he will speak out against the Most High and will wear down the saints of the Most High. . . . This person is known in the Bible as Antichrist.[5]

That's what our dispensationalist friends believe. In fact, the famous Baptist preacher Jerry Falwell has reportedly announced on national television that the Antichrist has already been born and is silently being prepared for his nefarious end-time role in prophecy. They believe we're that close to the end.

And when (after the secret rapture) the Antichrist signs a treaty with Israel, he will rule the world for seven long years of tribulation, in the middle of which, he will break his covenant with Israel, will be killed, will be resurrected from the dead by the devil, and will at last plunge earth into a final three and a half years of great tribulation. Then Jesus Christ will return a "third" time and finally destroy the wicked Antichrist. So teaches "Left Behind."

Will the Real Antichrist Please Stand Up?

But is the Antichrist of "Left Behind" and evangelical dispensationalism the Antichrist of Holy Scripture? Open your Bible and examine the evidence for yourself. For there is no question that the Bible teaches there is an Antichrist. But who is he, where is he, when is he—and is he a he?

Let's go to the very passage that "Left Behind" hopes will support its teaching that the Antichrist is yet to come in the near future.[6] 2 Thessalonians 2. But I warn you—this is a most dangerous truth. Because if the Bible does not teach that Jesus will return to this earth secretly to rapture His church (and we have shown that clearly the Bible does not teach that) . . . and if the Bible does not teach that after the secret rapture those who are left behind have seven more years to get ready for His third coming (and we have shown that clearly the Bible does not teach that, either) . . . then that means that there is no future seven-year tribulation in which any Antichrist can rule. So if we're not to look to the future for the prophesied Antichrist, then could it be that the Antichrist has already come . . . and is already here?

What Did Paul Say?

Let's read Paul's stunning teaching on the Antichrist. He begins:

> Now we request you, brethren, with regard to the *coming* of our Lord Jesus Christ and our gathering together to Him, that you not be quickly shaken from your composure or be disturbed either by a spirit or a message or a letter as if from us, to the effect that the day of the Lord has come.[7]

And with that Paul plunges into a discussion about the second coming of Christ. And he uses the code word that all early Christians know refers to Jesus' "coming" the second time: *parousia* (Greek). It's the same word the disciples used with Jesus when they asked: "What will be the sign of your *coming* and the end of the age?"[8]

Paul, in 2 Thessalonians 2, is clearly describing the second advent of Christ. And he describes it as our being "gathered together to Him." Those are significant words to dispensationalists who teach the "secret rapture." You see, they point out, when the *parousia* or coming of Christ occurs, all believers are "gathered together to Him" and are taken back to heaven. And we can agree! It's just that neither *parousia* nor "gathered together to Him" offer even a remote hint of anything secret or stealthful. However, we can at least all agree—and this is a vital point, as you will see in just a moment—that this passage is indeed describing the second coming of Jesus.

Let's reread Paul's opening line for one other important point:

> Now we request you, brethren, with regard to the coming of our Lord Jesus Christ and our gathering together to Him, that you not be quickly shaken from your composure or be disturbed either by a spirit or a message or a letter as if from us, to the effect that the day of the Lord has come.[9]

Chill, Everybody!

In other words, "I hear that some of you are worried that we have been going around preaching and teaching that Jesus has already returned! Relax, my friends [or as my teenage daughter Kristin would exclaim, 'Take a chill pill'], for that is *not* the case at all."

And then to support his assurance that the "day of the Lord"—the second coming of Christ—has not already transpired, Paul reminds his readers of a most dangerous and urgent prophecy that must first be fulfilled *before* Jesus will come again!

> Let no one in any way deceive you, for it will not come unless the apostasy comes first, and the man of lawlessness is revealed, the son of destruction, who opposes and exalts himself above every so-called god or object of worship, so that he takes his seat in the temple of God, displaying himself as being God.[10]

Paul ardently responds, "Jesus *cannot* come, until the ominous prophecies about the Antichrist first come true!"

But you say, "Wait a minute! I don't read a word about the Antichrist in those lines." And you are right.

Actually, the word *antichrist* is used only five times in the Bible—and all five times are in the New Testament. In order to understand who or what "antichrist" means in the Bible, we need to take a quick diversion from Paul and read the words of John, since all five instances are in his epistles. Note them carefully—five uses of the word that help identify the Antichrist:

•

1 JOHN 2:18—"Children, it is the last hour; and just as you heard that antichrist is coming, even now many antichrists have appeared; from this we know that it is the last hour" (NASB).

KEY POINT #1—"Antichrist" is not only singular—it also is plural. That means it cannot be confined to a single human being. So there can be more than one manifestation of this antichrist spirit.

•

1 JOHN 2:22—"Who is the liar but the one who denies that Jesus is the Christ? This is the antichrist, the one who denies the Father and the Son" (NASB).

KEY POINT #2—The Greek word *antichristos* means "instead of Christ." We often think of "anti" as "against." But in this case anyone or anything that seeks to become "instead of Christ" would certainly end up becoming "against Christ." The "antichrist" in this text denies the role of Jesus in the community of faith, even going so far as to deny the Father as well.

•

1 JOHN 2:26—"These things I have written to you concerning those who are trying to deceive you."

KEY POINT #3—In following up his first three references to Aantichrist," John clearly identifies deception as the predominant *modus operandi* of an "antichrist."

•

1 JOHN 4:2, 3—"By this you know the Spirit of God: every spirit that confesses that Jesus Christ has come in the flesh is from God; and every spirit that does not confess Jesus is not from God; and this is the spirit of the **antichrist**, of which you have heard that it is coming, and now it is already in the world" (NASB).

KEY POINT #4—The "antichrist" was already in the world when John wrote these words at the end of the first century A.D. Which means "Left Behind" cannot be right in attempting to relegate the Antichrist to the end of time *after* the secret second coming of Christ! Dispensationalists are simply but clearly wrong. Already in John's day, the Christian Church is witnessing the stealthful infiltration of the antichrist spirit!

•

2 JOHN 7—"For many deceivers have gone out into the world, those who do not acknowledge Jesus Christ as coming in the flesh. This is the deceiver and the **antichrist**" (NASB).

KEY POINT #5—The "antichrist" clearly begins in the church but in the end through deception actually leads its followers into the darkness of the world.

•

There they are—the Bible's five references to "antichrist" give us five significant keys to understanding who or what this Antichrist power is:

#1—It cannot be a single man—for it is plural.

#2—It seeks to usurp the place of the Son and the Father.

#3—It works by deception.

#4—It was already at work in the time of the early church.

#5—It begins in the church, but through deception leads its followers into the world.

Can you see that from John's statements alone that the "Left Behind" theory loses biblical credibility when it asserts that the Bible Antichrist is a future appearance of a single evil man? The Antichrist is not some unique future appearance, for nineteen centuries ago John declared it to be already present. It is not a single individual or man, for John declares it to be a manifold plural manifestation. It is not pagan, for John declares it to be a deception that is born and bred in the bosom of Christianity.

Consequently, "Left Behind" has left behind the most dangerous truth of all. For while its authors keep pointing to the future, it turns out that stealthfully, the Antichrist is already thoroughly entrenched in both the past and the present of Christianity!

Let's return now to Paul and discover that indeed with crystal and clarion precision he and John are in perfect agreement regarding the dangerous truth about the Antichrist. We have noted John's five key points; now let's examine Paul's three key identifying points about the Antichrist—truth we dare not miss:

•

"Let no one in any way deceive you, for *it* [the *parousia* or second coming of Jesus in the previous verse] *will not come* unless the apostasy comes first, and the man of lawlessness [Antichrist] is revealed, the son of destruction."[11]

KEY POINT #1—The great apostasy of the Antichrist must come *before* the second coming of Christ.

•

Paul will carefully identify the Antichrist in his second key point (which we will note soon). But here at the outset Paul outlines the critical sequence for *when* the Antichrist is to appear.

Since "Left Behind" also recognizes the Antichrist in this passage, it would behoove "Left Behind" then to learn from the very passage it quotes. For Paul is clear: The Antichrist must appear *before* the *parousia* (which "Left Behind" describes in verse 1 as the secret rapture). "Left Behind" and dispensationalism have made a terrible mistake. They are looking for the Antichrist to come some time in the future *after* the *parousia*, when all the while Paul could not be clearer: The Antichrist comes *before* the second coming of Jesus.

Paul doubles his point by remaking it in verse 8: "Then that lawless one [Antichrist] will be revealed whom the Lord will slay with the breath of His mouth and bring to an end by the appearance of His coming [*parousia*]" (NASB). Paul declares that it will be the second coming of Jesus that brings forever to an end the rule of the Antichrist.

But please note this critical distinction. Paul uses in verse 8 the very same word for the second coming of Jesus that he used in verse 1: *parousia*. Our "Left Behind" friends want the *parousia* in verse 1 to describe the "secret rapture." But in a dramatic and illogical shift, they try to tell us that the *parousia* in verse 8 is actually Christ's "third" coming, or "glorious appearing" (to use LaHaye's phrase). But by what stretch of logic do they force the very word they say is the "secret rapture" in verse 1 into also becoming the very "un-secret" rapture of verse 8! These "secret rapture" theorists simply cannot have it both ways—or they make a mockery of Paul and of the Bible's consistent use of *parousia*. In order to accommodate their theory, they have sadly turned *parousia,* the New Testament's glorious word for the second coming of Christ, into a rubber nose that they twist and turn in an effort to force it to fit with a mistaken theology and a misguided eschatology (biblical end-time teaching).

If we abide by the Bible and Paul's consistency, then it is utterly clear that the Antichrist must appear before *the second coming* (parousia) *of Christ.* As we noted above, that is precisely the point John also makes about the *antichristos.* The New Testament evidence is incontrovertibly clear: the Antichrist exercises his dominion and power *before* Jesus returns.

Which simply means "Left Behind" has left behind the truth about the Antichrist. And what a dangerous truth to leave behind!

Now let us examine Paul's second key point—the identity of the Antichrist.

•

"Let no one in any way deceive you, for *it* [the *parousia* or second coming of Jesus in the previous verse] *will not come* unless the apostasy comes first, and the man of lawlessness [Antichrist] is revealed, the son of destruction."[12]

KEY POINT #2—The Antichrist is inside the church of Christ, not outside.

•

Note carefully the three terms Paul uses to describe the Antichrist power: the apostasy, the man of lawlessness (some translations, "the man of sin"), and the son of destruction (some translations, "son of perdition").

Take that last identification, "the son of perdition." Do you remember reading that phrase in a well-known Bible story? Jesus actually spoke that phrase on the eve of His crucifixion. In fact, He prayed those words when He was praying for His disciples: "While I was with them, I was keeping them in Your name which You have given Me; and I guarded them and not one of them perished but the son of perdition, so that the Scripture would be fulfilled."[13] Jesus calls His betrayer, Judas, "the son of perdition."

It is significant that Paul takes the very words of Jesus, describing an internal ("inside job") traitor, to identify the Antichrist power that would be manifest before Christ returns. Paul's point? The Antichrist would do its nefarious work, all the while cloaked within the community of Christ.

"Left Behind" tries to depict the Antichrist as some godless, pagan evil man who will one day appear. But both Paul and John are adamant in their declaration that the Antichrist is a traitor power within or inside the Church, the community of Christ.

That point is inescapable in the very next verse: "Who opposes and exalts himself above every so-called god or object of worship, so that he takes his seat in the temple of God, displaying himself as being God."[14]

Talking about *anti*-Christ, or "instead of" Christ, here is a power that exalts itself above every "object of worship" (which would include Christ Jesus), even usurping His seat in the "temple of God."

"Left Behind" sadly tries to turn that phrase into a prediction that a third temple would be rebuilt one day in Jerusalem, and that into that rebuilt temple the Antichrist (an evil, pagan man) will take his seat. But that theory simply doesn't work. Because when Paul uses the phrase "temple of God," he is always referring to the community or church of Christ, never the Jerusalem temple.[15] Thus, by the phrase "temple of God" Paul reiterates his point that the Antichrist would appear within the community of Christ. I repeat: both Paul and John are absolute in their declaration that the Antichrist is a traitor power inside the Church.

And when will the Antichrist power appear? Paul finishes his description with yet another significant identifier.

•

"Do you not remember that while I was still with you, I was telling you these things? And you know what restrains him now, so that in his time he will be revealed. For the mystery of lawlessness is already at work; only he who now restrains *will do so* until he is taken out of the way."[16]

KEY POINT #3—The Antichrist is unleashed when the Roman empire collapses.

•

Paul now must very carefully choose his words. He is writing to a fledgling community of Christians inside the Roman Empire. They are already experiencing persecution at the hands of the Roman power, as Paul noted earlier in this letter.[17] Therefore, Paul dare not risk suggesting or fostering any anti-Roman sentiment within the infant Christian church. Certainly not in writing, anyway. Although he here alludes to something he has already preached to them when they were together. "Remember what I told you when we were together?" Whatever it was, he can only cryptically refer to it. What teaching could it have been?

Paul, as a faithful Jewish Christian, was obviously well schooled in the apocalyptic book of Daniel. No doubt he had taught his young disciples its dramatic prophecies. While he cannot risk referencing the Roman Empire in writing, his language here in 2 Thessalonians 2 clearly parallels the ominous description in Daniel 7, wherein Daniel prophesies the collapse of the Roman Empire and the subsequent dramatic rise of the Antichrist power, described by Daniel as a "little horn" with eyes and a mouth like a man.

Here is Daniel's prophecy:

> And four great beasts were coming up from the sea, different from one another. . . . I approached one of those who were standing by and began asking him the exact meaning of all this. So he told me and made known to me the interpretation of these things: "These great beasts, which are four *in number,* are four kings *who* will arise from the earth." . . . Then I desired to know the exact meaning of the . . . that horn which had eyes and a mouth uttering great *boasts,* and which was larger in appearance than its associates. I kept looking, and that horn was waging war with the saints and overpowering them. . . .

> He said: "The fourth beast will be a fourth kingdom on the earth, which will be different from all the *other* kingdoms, and it will devour the whole earth and tread it down and crush it. As for the ten horns, out of this kingdom ten kings will arise; and another will arise after them, and he will be different from the previous ones and will subdue three kings. And he will speak out against the Most High and wear down the saints of the Highest One, and he will intend to make alterations in times and in law; and they will be given into his hand for a time, times, and half a time. But the court will sit *for judgment,* and his dominion will be taken away, annihilated and destroyed forever."[18]

It is not our place here to extensively examine this great apocalyptic prophecy of Daniel. Many scholars identify the four beasts of Daniel's vision with the four empires of Babylon, Medo-Persia, Greece and Rome.

More intriguing to us all, as it certainly was for Daniel, is the identity of this "little horn" power that mysteriously arises out of the ashes of the collapsed fourth or Roman Empire. What is this "little horn" power that would ruthlessly "wear down the saints" of God for a period of "three and a half times"—which in Revelation 12:6 and 14 is calculated to be three and a half prophetic years or

1,260 prophetic days or (using the "day for a year" prophetic measuring stick) 1,260 years? What is this "little horn" power that would hold such crushing political as well as religious sway over the people of God for more than a millennium in history—a period we still remember as the Dark Ages and Middle Ages? Who is this "little horn" power—this "apostasy"—this "man of lawlessness"—this "son of perdition" that would become a traitor to the very community of Christ that it occupied? Who is this power that "takes his seat in the temple of God, displaying himself as being God"?

A half millennium ago there was no question who this power really was!

The Antichrist Identified

In 1528 in the quaint German town of Wittenberg, Martin Luther—the one man about whom more books have been written than any other religious figure outside of Jesus Christ—republished a commentary on the book of Revelation. It had been written one hundred-forty years earlier by John Purvey, an Englishman and follower of the English Reformer John Wycliffe. In the preface to this reprinted commentary, Martin Luther wrote:

> This preface, noble reader, you may understand was written by us for this reason—that we might make known to the world that we are not the first to interpret the Papacy as the kingdom of the Antichrist. For many years prior to us, so many and so great men (whose number is large, and their memory eternal) have attempted this so clearly and openly, and that with great spirit and force, that [those] who were driven by the fury of the papal tyranny into the farthest boundaries of the earth, and suffering the most atrocious tortures, nevertheless bravely and faithfully persisted in the confession of the truth.[19]

What was that truth for which "so great men . . . bravely and faithfully persisted" to confess? It is the very truth "Left Behind" has left behind: the truth of the Antichrist. And who is that Antichrist so fearlessly identified by Daniel and Paul and John?

A half millennium ago there was no question who this power really was!

Listen to the words of the Westminster Confession of Faith, ratified by the British Parliament in 1647:

> There is no other head of the Church but the Lord Jesus Christ: nor can the Pope of Rome, in any sense be head thereof; but is that Antichrist, that man of sin and son of perdition, that exalteth himself in the church against Christ, and all that is called God.[20]

Who is this power that Daniel and Paul and John all prophesied would rule Christendom and eventually the world before the return of Christ?

Read the words of Michael de Semlyen:

> Wycliffe, Tyndale, Luther, Calvin, Cranmer; in the seventeenth century, Bunyan, the translators of the King James Bible, and the men who published the Westminster and Baptist Confessions of Faith; Sir Isaac Newton, John Wesley, Whitfield, Jonathan Edwards; and more recently, Spurgeon, Bishop J. C. Ryle, and Dr. Martin Lloyd-Jones; these men among countless others, all saw the office of the Papacy as the antichrist.[21]

Do you know that means? It means that "Left Behind" is unwittingly a dangerous smoke screen that cloaks the very truth that the blood of the Reformers and the sacrifice of the martyrs unmasked. And that is the truth that the Antichrist is not someone yet to come—but that it is a power already come—for it is already here today. And beneath the folds of its ecclesiastical robes lies hidden the deadly sword that shall yet be plunged into the heart of earth's last civilization.

A Power, Not a Person

Already the Apocalypse is coming true: "The whole earth followed the beast [Antichrist]."[22]

So whom will *you* follow?

It may be that you are discovering this truth for the first time in your life right now. If so, you need to know that the truth about the Antichrist is not a truth about you or me or any one else. For it is not a truth about any *person*—a neighbor or a coworker or a friend—but rather the truth about a *power*. It is not a truth about *individuals,* but rather the sad but scriptural truth about an *institution*—a religious-political institution that tragically over the centuries of Christianity has exchanged the faith of Jesus for an eclectic syncretism that has combined pagan ritual with Christian tradition.

As a consequence, this institution has become the prophetic personification of that which opposes God and His law. For that reason, the Apocalypse cries out to the innocent adherents within the folds of this religion today: "Come out of her, my people."[23]

Jesus is coming soon. It is high time for you and me to decide whom we will follow. And so I earnestly appeal to you: Don't take my word for a single truth. But take the Holy Scripture, and with renewed passion and purpose, reexamine its living truths. Claim this promise of God to reveal to you the truths that have been left behind: "Call to me and I will answer you, and will tell you great and hidden things that you have not known."[24] Call upon God, and He will send you His Spirit to teach you. You have the word of Jesus on that: "When the Spirit of truth comes, He will guide you into all the truth."[25]

Martin Luther, who once stood all alone before the Antichrist power and defended his faith in the Word of God, cried out: "Here I stand, I can do no other; may God help me. Amen."

And may the God of Daniel and Paul and John and Martin Luther help you and me to do the same. For we can do no other.

"Even so, come, Lord Jesus."

Notes:

[1] *The Arizona Republic,* January 31, 2001.

[2] *Wall Street Journal,* February 1, 2001.

[3] Fax from Namesake Entertainment to Christian media outlets,

February 7, 2001.

[4]Tim LaHaye and Jerry B. Jenkins, *Left Behind,* p. 448.

[5]Tim Lahaye and Jerry B. Jenkins, *Are We Living in the End Times?* pp. 271, 272.

[6]I am indebted to Steve Wohlberg's studies of 2 Thessalonians 2 and 1 and 2 John in his books, *Exploding the Israel Deception and Truth Left Behind.*

[7]2 Thessalonians 2:1, 2, NASB, emphasis supplied.

[8]Matthew 24:3—*parousia* also appears in 1 Thessalonians 2:19, 4:15; 5:23; and James 5:7.

[9]2 Thessalonians 2:1, 2, NASB.

[10]2 Thessalonians 2:3, 4, NASB.

[11]2 Thessalonian 2:3.

[12]*Ibid.*

[13]John 17:12, NASB.

[14]2 Thessalonians 2:4, NASB.

[15]1 Corinthians 3:16; 2 Corinthians 6:16; Ephesians 2:19-21. In one instance, Paul uses the "temple of God" metaphor to refer to our bodies—1 Corinthians 6:19.

[16]2 Thessalonians 2:5-7, NASB.

[17]See 2 Thessalonians 1:4.

[18]Daniel 7:3, 16, 17, 23-26, NASB.

[19]Quoted in L. E. Froom, *Prophetic Faith of Our Fathers,* vol. 2, p. 94.

[20]Phillip Schaff, *The Creeds of Christendom-With a History and Critical Notes,* vol. 3, pp. 658, 659.

[21]Michael de Semlyen, *All Roads Lead to Rome,* pp. 205, 206.

[22]Revelation 13:3.

[23]Revelation 18:4.

[24]Jeremiah 33:3.

[25]John 16:13.

The Most Compelling Truth of All

HERE'S SOMETHING TO PONDER: Is a warning good news—or bad news?

An incident took place in San Diego recently that became the second such occurrence in the Southwest. A woman went into a nursery and purchased a large cactus plant as part of the redecoration of her home. The huge cactus was a fitting centerpiece for her "New Southwest" decor. And she was quite happy with her $3,000 purchase . . . for a while. Until a few days later when she noticed that the big cactus seemed to be swaying . . . and then she got up close to it and realized it was humming!

Bewildered and not knowing where else to turn, she dialed 9-1-1. Fortunately for her, she got an operator who knew what this uncactus-like behavior meant. The operator's warning was clear and firm: "Ma'am, you must evacuate your house immediately—and wait outside for an emergency team." The responding five-man team had just enough time to lift the huge cactus out of the house and into the backyard. Whereupon it burst wide open, scattering a thousand tarantulas in all directions! The nursery she had purchased the cactus from refunded her $3,000 and paid for exterminator service for the entire block! When asked later how her plants were doing, the woman replied, "Plastic and silk, thank you!"

The fashion of using cacti for home decoration is fairly new. But apparently tarantulas have been using them for mass breeding farms for a very long time.

Question: Is a warning good news or bad news?

Answer: There is a woman today in San Diego who is deeply grateful for the warning of that 911 operator.

And there are three naval commanders who, I am certain, would give about anything they had, if only someone had warned them that sitting helplessly in their submarine's upward trajectory was a hapless, crowded Japanese fishing vessel, which they would tragically sink to the bottom of the sea.

Question: Is a warning good news or bad news?

Answer: The victims of killer quakes and devastating aftershocks in northwest India and El Salvador will to a man and woman and child tell you that they would have given anything if only they could have been warned of impending disaster!

In anybody's book anywhere on this planet, it is true: A warning of impending disaster is always very good news. *If* the warning is heeded.

Urgent Warning

Come with me then to a warning one author has called "the most fearful threatening ever addressed to mortals": Revelation 14. The urgent messages of three midnight angels. There is no more threatening warning than what you are about to read. But remember, if a warning is good news, then we have every reason to be very glad for this one.

Which is why I am utterly nonplussed that there is not even a hint of this most compelling truth of all in the "Left Behind" books and movie. What is even more troubling is that "Left Behind" has inadvertently advocated the very opposite of this warning truth. And the very opposite of truth in anybody's book is falsehood.

How can we know the difference? Let's go to the Book and discover what "Left Behind" has left behind this time: the most compelling truth of all.

> Then I saw another angel flying in the midst of heaven, having the everlasting gospel to preach to those who dwell on the earth— to every nation, tribe, tongue, and people—saying with a loud voice, "Fear God and give glory to Him, for the hour of His judgment has come; and worship Him who made heaven and earth, the sea and springs of water."
>
> And another angel followed, saying, "Babylon is fallen, is fallen, that great city, because she has made all nations drink of the wine of the wrath of her fornication."
>
> Then a third angel followed them, saying with a loud voice, "If anyone worships the beast and his image, and receives his mark on his forehead or on his hand, he himself shall also drink of the wine of the wrath of God, which is poured out full strength into the cup of His indignation. He shall be tormented with fire and brimstone in the presence of the holy angels and in the presence of the Lamb. And the smoke of their torment ascends forever and ever; and they have no rest day or night, who worship the beast and his image, and whoever receives the mark of his name.
>
> Here is the patience of the saints; here are those who keep the commandments of God and the faith of Jesus.[1]

Angelic Flyovers

Here is a message pertinent for America, since we're a nation consumed with speed! Internet speed, highway speed, race track speed—we love to live at full throttle. The tragic death of Dale Earnhardt at the Daytona 500 early in 2001 is but a somber reminder of the lengths to which we'll go in order to vicariously experience the high-flying adrenalin of speed.

The aged prophet John hears something and looks up just in time to witness an angel at full celestial throttle streaking across the midnight heavens. Not at treetop level, like a radar-evading

F-15 fighter jet, mind you, or somewhere out in nether space like the Space Shuttle—this angel flies like a comet in "midheaven," as one translation puts it. And John is transfixed.

Because no sooner has the elderly prophet experienced one fly-over by that angel, then there are two more angelic fly-overs in quick succession. Three midnight angels, with what is God's final, passionate appeal and warning to a civilization living at the edge and end of time.

That must explain why this warning isn't whispered! In the Greek the "loud voice" of the first angel and the third angel is *megale phone,* from whence comes our word "megaphone." The messages of these angels are megaphoned as loud as possible to earth's inhabitants at the end of time!

How can we know this is near the end? Look at the glorious scene that John gazed upon as soon as the three angels were finished: "Then I looked, and behold, a white cloud, and on the cloud sat One like the Son of Man, having on His head a golden crown, and in His hand a sharp sickle."[2] Clearly then, we are eaves-dropping on the final apocalyptic warning and appeal of the God of the universe to this planet in rebellion!

Mark of the Beast

How did that author describe this warning? "The most fearful threatening ever addressed to mortals is contained in the third angel's message."[3] A quick glance back to that third angel's message will reveal that it is a warning against "the mark of the beast."

Interestingly enough, the "Left Behind" series is intrigued with this "mark of the beast" in the forehead or in the hand. So much so, in fact, that the eighth volume in what will eventually be a twelve-volume series is entitled *The Mark (The Beast Rules the World).* But quite frankly, they shouldn't be the only ones intrigued with this "mark of the beast."

When was the last time you ever took it seriously? Oh, we've heard it laughed about in the press and snickered about in some

Christian circles. But, my friend, if this is indeed the "most fearful threatening" and warning "ever addressed to mortals"—and if a life-saving warning is always good news—then you and I, for the sake of saving our lives, had better get the news straight! Straight from the Word of God.

Final Cosmic Showdown

Fascinatingly enough, the Apocalypse portrays a not-so-subtle play and counterplay between the "mark of the beast" and the "mark of God." Both sides in the final cosmic showdown mark their loyal adherents. The Antichrist power marks its followers in two places. God marks His friends in only one place. But both warring sides, both battling forces, are desperately intent on identifying which earthlings are in fact loyal to their kingdom.

But the only way we can understand the meaning of the "mark of the beast" is to first examine and understand the "mark of God." Fortunately for us, the Bible is compellingly clear on God's mark.

In fact, just before the Apocalypse records God's last passionate appeal to earth, the verses immediately preceding the three angels paint a portrait of the earth inhabitants who accept God's final warning and embrace Him in earth's final apocalyptic showdown:

> Then I looked, and behold, a Lamb [the dominant symbol for Christ in Revelation] standing on Mount Zion, and with Him one hundred and forty-four thousand, having His Father's name written on their foreheads.[4]

Here is a portrait of the followers of Christ at the end of time. And did you notice? They are marked in only one place—their foreheads. Earlier we read that the followers of the Antichrist are marked in one of two places—the forehead or the hand. Why the difference? Simple. Because Christ and the Antichrist operate out of two very different universes—two very opposite worldviews.

The Antichrist doesn't care whether you intellectually embrace what that fallen religious-political power stands for or not. You may say Yes to it with your mind. Or you may only acquiesce to it and be led along by the hand, pulled along by the crowd. Whether you're following conviction or following the crowd, it doesn't matter to the Antichrist—as long as you follow. That's the way the devil has always played his game.

How many a little girl has said No in her mind, but has allowed that sweet-talking boy to lead her along by the hand? Happens all the time. How many grown-up adults, in order to be politically correct, or at least accepted in their department or at their office, have said No in their minds but have allowed the popular opinion to lead them along by the hand?

The Antichrist (a visible front for the dragon or devil)[5] doesn't care how you go along—as long as you go along.

But God cares. Which is why He refuses to mark any friend in the hand—only the free choice of the mind will do for Him. Because nobody follows the crowd into the kingdom of God. You *choose* to follow the Lamb, you *choose* to be a friend of God's, you *choose* to obey His Word no matter the cost. God has always known that without a choice, it's never love. And God can't image a friendship without love.

And so God's mark of loyalty goes only on the forehead. And what is that mark of His? Seven chapters earlier in the Apocalypse we are given the answer:

> After these things I saw four angels standing at the four corners of the earth, holding the four winds of the earth, that the wind should not blow on the earth, on the sea, or on any tree. Then I saw another angel ascending from the east, having the seal of the living God. And he cried with a loud voice to the four angels to whom it was granted to harm the earth and the sea, saying, "Do not harm the earth, the sea, or the trees till we have sealed the servants of our God on their foreheads."[6]

Once again we encounter an apocalyptic high-flying angel with a "loud voice"! I once ran into that *megale phone* ("megaphone") phrase so many times while reading Revelation that I decided to count how often Revelation gets loud. Twenty-one times! (Which I have very cheerfully shared with my wife, Karen—who thinks that stereos are supposed to be played at 1 and 2 on the volume knob! If that were the case, why did they invent 9 and 10 on that same knob? Since God enjoys His Apocalypse loud, I am comforted to learn that I can, too.)

God's Seal of Approval

And what does this ascending angel call the mark of God on the foreheads of His friends? "The seal of the living God." You see, God has the equivalent of a "Good Housekeeping Seal of Approval" that He stamps upon all His loyal and forever friends in earth's last generation! Perhaps it's like the Christmas gift Karen gave me one year—a nifty metal seal-maker that can literally emboss my name onto the cover pages of all my books. When I squeeze that chrome "sealer" along the edge of a page, it imprints a raised, indelible seal containing my name. God has a seal for the same reason—it's a sign that the one who is sealed belongs to Him!

So what is it that gets sealed in the foreheads or minds of God's friends? The Bible won't leave us in the dark on so vital an issue. "This is the covenant that I will make with them after those days, says the Lord: I will put My laws into their hearts, and in their minds I will write them."[7] To a generation living at the end of time, God cries out: "Hold back the winds of destruction—let Me first write My Law upon the minds [foreheads] of My followers and friends."

Does the Old Testament support this New Testament teaching? Yes it does. "Bind up the testimony, seal the law among my disciples,"[8] are God's instructions. Again, it is the Law that is sealed into hearts and minds of His friends. In fact, if this end-time generation is *not* sealed with God's Law, note very carefully His somber declaration: "To the law and to the testimony! If they do not speak according to this word, it is because there is no light in them."[9] No light in those who are not sealed with God's law in the end. That *is* a somber warning!

Let's be honest. Some Christians are very uncomfortable with

God being so big on His own Law, big on His Ten Commandments. But what's the problem? Or as the kids say, What's up with *that?* God ought to be big on the Law. After all, it's simply a shining reflection of His own character.

A few weeks ago one of our staff pastors—who shall remain nameless for obvious reasons—was apprehended by a policeman for not coming to a complete stop at the four-way stop sign on our campus. (I would have been happy to fulfill my Christian duty and visit him in jail had he ended up there.) Fortunately for our errant pastor, the officer was gracious to him and explained to him that the big red octagonal signs with S-T-O-P on them mean just that. It's the law. You must stop. The pastor came to me later and asked if I'd ever been stopped at that four-way stop sign—to which I replied with great humility and pride: Never in all my life!

But the reason our anonymous pastor will never forget that law and will always stop at that corner in the future is that the officer who pulled him over is one of our faithful parishioners. From now on, every time he approaches that four-way stop sign, Pastor X can picture the face of the Lawman as he remembers the force of the Law.

Law and Lawgiver

Which is the way it is with God's Law! The Lawgiver is at the very heart of the Law given. You cannot reject one without rejecting the other. Which means that not one of those Ten Commandments can be laid aside or disobeyed or even ignored—without casting aside the very Lawgiver whose reflection they are in the first place.

Amazingly enough, God's face shines the most brightly in one of the Ten Commandments. Do you know which one?

Before we turn to the Ten Commandments in Exodus 20, let me share a political cartoon I saw a few weeks ago that reflects the press's post-William Jefferson Clinton analysis of our former president and the swirl of controversy that still surrounds him. The pardons he issued on his last day in office, the gifts he and his wife took away from the White House—it hasn't been a very pretty scene.

One cartoonist decided to symbolize it all with the drawing of a pawnshop window in New York or some such city. And there in the window—obviously pawned off to the dealer—and now being offered to the highest bidder: the familiar eagle-graced United States presidential seal. The cartoonist's point was unsubtle—the presidential office itself has been pawned off.

Most of us are familiar with three components in the presidential seal: name, office, and jurisdiction. So our present president's seal would be stamped: Name—George Walker Bush; Office—President; Jurisdiction—United States of America. That's what typically makes an official seal.

In Search of a Seal

Does God have a seal? Remember what we have verified thus far in our study:

#1—God will seal His final forever friends with a seal in their forehead.

#2—God seals His followers with His Law.

#3—Therefore, somewhere in God's Law we shall be able to find God's seal.

And sure enough—one of the Ten Commandments contains the very seal of God. It is the Fourth Commandment:

> Remember the Sabbath day, to keep it holy. Six days you shall labor and do all your work, but the seventh day is the Sabbath of the Lord your God. In it you shall do no work: you, nor your son, nor your daughter, nor your male servant, nor your female servant, nor your cattle, nor your stranger who is within your gates. For in six days the Lord made the heavens and the earth, the sea, and all that is in them, and rested the seventh day. Therefore the Lord blessed the Sabbath day and hallowed it.[10]

Did you see the three components of God's seal in this commandment? Here they are: Name—"The Lord your God; Office—"Maker/Creator"; and Jurisdiction—"The Heavens and the Earth." There it is—in the heart of the Ten Commandments—the seal of God.

Which means God's Fourth Commandment—"Remember the seventh-day Sabbath to keep it holy"—is the very commandment that is sealed into the minds/foreheads of God's last generation of followers and friends.

And that is precisely what Revelation comes along and boldly announces: The final issue on this planet before the return of Christ will be the counterplay and showdown between the "seal of God" and the "mark of the beast."

Two—and No More

There will be only two camps at the end of time. Two warring kingdoms, two battling ideologies, two and only two sides to the entire human race. One side with the "seal of God" on the forehead—the other side with the "mark of the beast" on the forehead or on the hand. There will be no third mark. For there can be no third side.

Which is why the Apocalypse is so passionate about defining what it means to be on God's side with God's seal!

Remember how Revelation describes God's friends as being sealed with God's name in their foreheads?[11] Want to know by what name God is most often called in Revelation?

Revelation 4:10, 11—God is called the Creator, "for You created all things."

Revelation 10:5, 6—In language straight out of the fourth commandment, God is called the Creator of heaven and earth and the sea.

Revelation 14:6, 7—Again, with the actual wording straight out of the Septuagint (the Greek Old Testament) translation of the fourth commandment, God is called the Maker of heaven and earth and sea and fountains of water.

Over and over in the Apocalypse, God is named and worshiped as the almighty Creator of all life forms. And it is His name and His office and His jurisdiction that are sealed into the minds of His last generation of friends on earth. Thus the biblical evidence is compelling that at the end of time the final global controversy will swirl around God's authority as Creator of the human race. That is why the midnight angel streaks across earth's last sky crying out with a mighty megaphone: "Fear God, and give glory to him, for the hour of his judgment has come; and worship him who made heaven and earth, the sea and springs of waters."[12]

Any way you wish to cut it, the fourth commandment will be in the cross-hairs of earth's final apocalyptic showdown! A showdown between God the Creator and Antichrist the usurper. A showdown between the "seal of God" and the "mark of the beast." A showdown between worshiping the Creator on His day, and worshiping the Antichrist on his day.

God's day we know—for Jesus declared, "The Son of Man is also Lord of the Sabbath."[13] If the seventh-day Sabbath day is Christ's day, then what day is the Antichrist's day?

Who Changed the Day?

I have in my library a little orange booklet entitled, *The Convert's Catechism of Catholic Doctrine.* Inside it are the official imprimaturs to declare that the author and priest, Peter Geiermann, was given all the ecclesiastical blessing necessary for this book to speak for Rome. Note this intriguing exchange:

Q. Which day is the Sabbath day?

A. Saturday is the Sabbath day.

Q. Why do we observe Sunday instead of Saturday?

A. We observe Sunday instead of Saturday because the Catholic

Church, in the Council of Laodicea (A.D. 336), transferred the solemnity from Saturday to Sunday.[14]

Notice the teaching of another catechism, this one by priest and scholar, Richard Challoner:

> Q. Has the [Catholic] church power to make any alterations in the commandments of God?
>
> A. Instead of the seventh day, and other festivals appointed in the old law, the church has prescribed the Sundays and holy days to be set apart for God's worship; and these we are now obliged to keep in consequence of God's commandment, instead of the ancient Sabbath.[15]

Isn't it strange that you cannot find anywhere in Scripture God granting any human being or any human institution the right or prerogative to alter that which He wrote with His own finger in stone! Quite to the contrary, the Bible ends with this somber warning: "If anyone adds to these things, God will add to him the plagues that are written in this book; and if anyone takes away from the words of the book of this prophecy, God shall take away his part from the Book of Life."[16]

Proof by Circular Reasoning

Then from whence came the power and prerogative of Rome to tamper with God's eternal law? Consider yet one more catechism, this one by priest author Steven Keenan:

> Q. Have you any other way of proving that the church has power to institute festivals or precepts?
>
> A. Had she not such power, she could not have done that in which all modern religionists agree with her. She could not have substituted the observance of Sunday the first day of the week, for the observance of Saturday the seventh day, a change for which there is no Scriptural authority.[17]

In a breathtaking demonstration of circular reasoning, a spokesman for this geo-religio-political power declares: The proof the church has the power to change the Sabbath to Sunday is found in the church's changing the Sabbath to Sunday. Without a hint of divine permission—contrary to all this Book stands for. "He shall think to change times and laws"—Daniel's prophecy was absolutely right![18]

There you have it. The dramatic contrast between the seal of God and the mark of the beast could hardly be more pronounced!

◆ The authority of God versus the authority of man.

◆ The worship of God versus the worship of man.

◆ The seventh-day Sabbath versus the first-day Sunday.

◆ God's day and way versus man's day and way.

◆ The seal of God versus the mark of the beast.

I repeat: It is inescapable in the Apocalypse that the final defining global issue before the return of Jesus will be the authority and worship of the Creator through His Lordship of the Sabbath.

It is no coincidence that the academic world today is ruled and racked by scientific atheism, under the euphemisms of naturalism and Darwinism. Human intellectual history is headed straight for this cataclysmic showdown between the authority of the Creator and the authority of the pseudo-creator power man vests in himself.

It is no accident that postmodern society is rapidly post-Christian and post-Creator, with social atheism ruling the media and the masses through secularism, materialism, and hedonism—all without a Creator.

Why, it is as if some dark sinister power were desperately seeking to destroy every vestige and evidence of a benevolent Creator from our minds and our society!

Revelation has jabbed its apocalyptic finger hard against the chest of this proud third-millennial society—and we stand both exposed and identified by the divine Spirit two millennia in advance.

We stand warned this day of the impending showdown between Christ and the Antichrist.

And to all those who mutter, "You'll never get the seventh-day Sabbath into the headlines of the global media," I introduce as contrary evidence the nomination of Joseph Lieberman as vice-presidential candidate for the Democratic Party in A.D. 2000.

Nobody in the secular press, it seems, had heard of observing the Bible Sabbath from sundown Friday evening to sundown Saturday evening, as the Jews and Seventh-day Adventists do the world over. But literally overnight, the Sabbath became the talking point of a thousand editorials and news releases. Literally overnight, God's seventh-day Sabbath (because while the Jews haven't found Jesus, they have kept His Sabbath) was catapulted into national consciousness.

So you don't need to worry. When God's ready, overnight the world will be given the choice: the seal of God or the mark of the beast. One national calamity, one massive global collapse of some sort—and the powers that already be will spring into action.

"And all the world wondered after the beast."[19]

The Seal Versus the Mark

The Bible is clear: God's seventh-day Sabbath will be the final line of demarcation between the seal of God and the mark of the beast.

My friend, if you are hearing this Bible truth for the first time, you need to know that there isn't a human being on this planet who has the mark of the beast today. The apocalyptic issues are yet a few paces away from becoming a global showdown. Which is why *now* is such a critical time to choose to "worship Him who made heaven and earth." Please don't take my word for it. Take the Word of God and examine it prayerfully and carefully for yourself.

You can pray this very simple prayer: O God, please seal upon my mind Your eternal law, that I might follow Your will for the rest of my life.

Then of you, too, the final words of the Three Angels' Messages will be written and true: "Here is the patience of the saints; here are those who keep the commandments of God and the faith of Jesus."[20]

"Even so, come, Lord Jesus."

Notes:

[1]Revelation 14:6-12, NKJV. Unless otherwise indicated, all biblical references in this chapter will be from the *New King James Version.*

[2]Revelation 14:14.

[3]Ellen White, *The Great Controversy,* p. 449.

[4]Revelation 14:1.

[5]See Revelation 13:2, 4.

[6]Revelation 7:1-3.

[7]Hebrews 10:16.

[8]Isaiah 8:16.

[9]Isaiah 8:20.

[10]Exodus 20:8-11.

[11]Revelation 14:1.

[12]Revelation 14:7.

[13]Mark 2:28.

[14]Peter Geiermann, *The Convert's Catechism of Catholic Doctrine,* p. 50.

[15]Richard Challoner, *The Catholic Christian Instructed,* p. 211.

[16]Revelation 22:18, 19.

[17]Stephen Keenan, *A Doctrinal Catechism,* p. 174.

[18]Daniel 7:25, KJV.

[19]Revelation 13:3, KJV.

[20]Revelation 14:12.

WHAT "LEFT BEHIND" LEFT BEHIND:

The Most Shaking Truth of All

MY SECRETARY CAME FLYING into my office on a Wednesday afternoon with news that Seattle had just been struck by a 6.8 earthquake. She knows that my brother Greg—who moved to Seattle in January to plant a church in the very heart of that most secular of American cities—lives on the twenty-third floor of a downtown apartment high-rise.

I grabbed my cell phone and punched in Greg's code. When he answered the phone, I blurted out: "Are you alive?" Turns out he and his associate pastor, Shasta Burr, were at a pastors' meeting at the Washington Conference camp at Sunset Lake. And in fact, they were all kneeling in prayer when the earthquake hit.

I couldn't help thinking of what had happened to the early church in Acts 4—"And when they had prayed, the place where they were assembled together was shaken."[1]

"Did you think about that text, Greg?"

"We did, after we all raced outside!"

Traffic back into Seattle after the quake was jammed for miles. When Greg got back to his apartment, it was still standing, though the walls of that tall building were cracked. Apparently the brick facades of the city's older buildings took the worst of the beating. Fortunately for Seattle—this time—the quake was thirty-two miles underground.

A Great Earthquake

"And I beheld when he had opened the sixth seal, and, lo, there was a great earthquake."[2] Probably not a description of the 6.8 Richter scale temblor that hit Seattle. Probably not even a description of the killer quakes that have been rumbling and rolling through this earth recently—leaving in their trembling wakes stories of grief and shock and fear and death! Which means Revelation 6 probably isn't describing the 7.9 killer quake that flattened northwest India in January 2001 and left 30,000 dead and 200,000 homeless. It probably isn't predicting the two killer quakes—one of them 7.6—that back-to-back struck El Salvador (the name means "The Saviour"), along with a follow-up third major 6.1 temblor four minutes before Seattle shook.

Mike Jones wrote in a recent piece in the *Adventist Review:*

> In addition to hammering India and El Salvador, another 20 earthquakes rating at least 5 on the Richter scale shook Japan, Indonesia, New Zealand, Mexico, the Santa Cruz Islands, the Solomon Islands, Peru, the Pacific-Antarctic Ridge, and Alaska in a six-day period between January 23 and 29.[3]

After reading that, I decided I needed to check this out for myself. And he was right. My daughter Kristin found the website of the United States Geological Service with a listing of all the earthquakes that struck during the forty-eight hour period surrounding the Seattle quake. We counted 21 quakes on that list, with seven of them over 5.0. And that was for only a two-day period!

Tom Brokaw announced on *NBC Nightly News* that already in 2001 before the Seattle quake, there had been seven earthquakes 7.0 and higher.

And now poor Los Angeles, constructed upon eight faults, is facing an 80 percent chance that the "Big One" will strike it within the next twenty years. The odds are equally foreboding for the city of my birth, Tokyo, Japan.

So what's going on? But the more significant question is, Who's coming back?

Two thousand years ago, Jesus left this warning of what could be expected on earth prior to his return: "There will be great earthquakes, and in various places famines and plagues; and there will be dreadful portents and great signs from heaven."[4]

Once your mind has been sensitized by Christ's somber warning, you cannot help but sit up and wonder every time the earth is shaken: Is this yet another sign of His soon coming?

There was a time—let me be candid with you—when I wrote off all earthquakes and natural disasters as simply that—natural. You know—it's nature doing her usual thing. After all, you can expect this kind of rock-and-roll existence, living as we are on an earth with seismic plates and deep geographic faults. Tectonic shifts have been a way of life forever around this terrestrial ball.

Read the Signs

So I once surmised, until I began to reflect more deeply upon words of Scripture. I was disturbed to discover that Holy Scripture often describes earthquakes as seminal signs or seismic warnings or judgments directly from God. Signs, as it were, that the God of the universe is approaching the very precincts of this earth!

Isaiah, Amos, Haggai, John, Joel, Jesus—to a man they link the quaking and shaking of the earth with the judgment of God! You can't escape the linkage. Listen to Isaiah: "You will be punished by the LORD of hosts with thunder and earthquake and great noise, with storm and tempest and the flame of devouring fire."[5] It is as if inanimate creation recognizes what our sin-stupefied minds refuse

to acknowledge—the Creator is approaching this fallen system—
He is about to return in person!

At the beginning of this past century, these warning words were
written:

> More and more, as the days go by, it is becoming apparent that
> God's judgments are in the world. In fire and flood and earth-
> quake He is warning the inhabitants of this earth of His near
> approach. The time is nearing when the great crisis in the history of
> the world will have come, when every movement in the government
> of God will be watched with intense interest and inexpressible
> apprehension. In quick succession the judgments of God will fol-
> low one another—fire and flood and earthquake, with war and
> bloodshed.[6]

Seven 7.0 earthquakes just in the first few weeks of 2001—could
it be that God is desperately trying to awaken this judgment-
bound civilization? Seattle partied mindlessly late into the night
the previous Saturday with a ribald and riotous Mardi Gras party
that became a destructive riot seen on national news. The next
Wednesday, she was shaken to the core.

"And I beheld when he had opened the sixth seal, and, lo, there
was a great earthquake. . . . For the great day of his wrath is come;
and *who shall be able to stand?*"[7]

It is no coincidence that the very next words in the Apocalypse
answer the initially troubling question, "Who shall be able to
stand?" To the question—Is there nobody who will stand?—comes
the glad and ringing response: Oh, yes, there is—there will be
thousands upon thousands upon thousands—hallelujah!—who
will stand in that Day when Jesus soon comes!

We are now in the heart of our final exploration of what "Left
Behind" left behind. So please keep reading. Don't stop with chapter
six. Because there's chapter seven!

> After these things I saw four angels standing at the four corners
> of the earth, holding the four winds of the earth, that the wind
> should not blow on the earth, on the sea, or on any tree. Then I
> saw another angel ascending from the east, having the seal of the

living God. And he cried with a loud voice to the four angels to whom it was granted to harm the earth and the sea, saying, "Do not harm the earth, the sea, or the trees till we have sealed the servants of our God on their foreheads." And I heard the number of those who were sealed. One hundred and forty-four thousand of all the tribes of the children of Israel were sealed.[8]

Who shall be able to stand in that great judgment day? Who will be ready for Jesus to come? Hallelujah—they shall stand by the thousands and thousands and thousands!

144,000—and No More?

Oh, really now—you ask—do you mean only 144,000 will stand and be ready in the end? Not at all. Because the Apocalypse doesn't mean that either.

Now, I must tell you that the "Left Behind" books are really big on trying to teach the world that these 144,000 are literal Jews who have converted to Christ sometime between the secret rapture and the end of the great seven-year tribulation.

I pulled out Tim LaHaye's companion volume, *Are We Living in the End Times?*—and page after page is devoted to trying to make this passage mean 144,000 Jewish witnesses (or evangelists). There's nothing wrong with Jewish witnesses, you understand; I have friends who are Jews and who are witnesses. But Tim LaHaye is trying hard to defend a brand of mistaken Bible interpretation called dispensationalism, which believes that all prophecies concerning Israel must be taken literally (which we have learned in chapter 4 is not true). So he has no choice but to conclude these are 144,000 Jewish witnesses.

In reality, though he doesn't mention this, a literal reading of Revelation's words necessitates that these are Jewish men.

You see, "Left Behind" left behind a critical parallel passage to this one, right here in the Apocalypse—and because they did, they left behind the truth.

Turn seven chapters further, to Revelation 14, for it is essential that Revelation 7:1-4 be joined with its parallel, Revelation 14:1-5, whose opening scene is: "Then I looked, and behold, a Lamb standing on Mount Zion, and with Him one hundred and forty-four thousand, having His Father's name written on their foreheads." We have been to these words before. And what a heavenly scene! Gathered around Jesus (the "Lamb" is a frequent apocalyptic symbol for the post-Calvary Christ) are His forever friends who remained loyal to Him on earth to the very end. But now at last they are shown in heaven. It reads "Mt. Zion," but that's simply a code name for heaven itself: "But you have come to Mount Zion and to the city of the living God, the heavenly Jerusalem, to an innumerable company of angels."[9] Jesus and His friends in heaven at last—what a glorious scene to look forward to!

But who are these friends of His, and will there be only 144,000 of them? Not at all! For the number is just as symbolic as the description of this end-time generation you're about to read:

> And I heard a voice from heaven, like the voice of many waters, and like the voice of loud thunder. And I heard the sound of harpists playing their harps. They sang as it were a new song before the throne, before the four living creatures, and the elders; and no one could learn that song except the hundred and forty-four thousand who were redeemed from the earth. These are the ones who were not defiled with women, for they are virgins. These are the ones who follow the Lamb wherever He goes. These were redeemed from among men, being firstfruits to God and to the Lamb. And in their mouth was found no deceit, for they are without fault before the throne of God.[10]

Did you catch it? These 144,000 are described as "virgins" who "were not defiled with women." Wait a minute! Does that mean that the people who are able to stand for God through to the cataclysmic end of time will be virgins? Well, that's what you'd have to conclude if you were forced to interpret this passage literally! In fact, a literal reading of Revelation 7 and 14 would mean that the 144,000 will all be virgin male Jews.[11] Which would leave a whole lot of us out of the picture! But fortunately "Left Behind" is what has left something out of the picture.

Then what does it mean when the Apocalypse describes this end-time generation as being "not defiled with women"? Let's note first what it does *not* mean. For it cannot mean that the 144,000 are all unmarried virgins. Simply because the Bible is clear: when a man marries a woman he is not defiled by her, as a literal interpretation of this text would suggest. Marriage is not defiling: "Marriage is honorable among all, and the bed undefiled."[12] Let us be clear—marriage between a man and a woman has been God's gift from the very beginning—it is not defiling. It is the marriage bed—or the sexual covenant between a husband and a wife—that you must keep *un*defiled. So John can hardly be trying to teach us that the 144,000 are unmarried virgin male Jews "undefiled" by any wife!

And what about the specific reference to the twelve tribes of Israel in Revelation 7:4-8? As already explained in chapter 4, the New Testament identity of Israel embraces God's global community of faith beyond all tribal identities and geographic boundaries. Therefore the twelve sealed tribes of Israel, referred to in Revelation 7, are a symbol of God's end-time community of faith.

In fact, references to male virgins, to Israel, and to the 144.000 are highly symbolic. The number 144,000 is but the squaring of one of the Bible's favorite numerals—twelve (as in the twelve tribes, twelve disciples, twelve foundations and twelve gates to the New Jerusalem, etc.)—and then increasing it a thousand fold. And the description of unmarried male virgins is symbolic of a deep truth.

A Tale of Two Women

A much more dramatic truth, the Apocalypse is portraying here—a truth "Left Behind" left behind. You see, there are actually two women portrayed in the Apocalypse. And what the book of Revelation exposes is a powerful play and counterplay—a high drama dialectic or tension—between these two women. Once you've been introduced to the two women, it suddenly clicks—the 144,000 are those people at the end of time who are not defiled by one of those two. They refuse to go to bed with her! Which one?

Let's share the brief but stunning portraits of both women in the Apocalypse:

> Now a great sign appeared in heaven: a woman clothed with the sun, with the moon under her feet, and on her head a garland of twelve stars. Then being with child, she cried out in labor and in pain to give birth. And another sign appeared in heaven: behold, a great, fiery red dragon having seven heads and ten horns, and seven diadems on his heads. His tail drew a third of the stars of heaven and threw them to the earth. And the dragon stood before the woman who was ready to give birth, to devour her Child as soon as it was born. She bore a male Child who was to rule all nations with a rod of iron. And her Child was caught up to God and His throne.

> Then the woman fled into the wilderness, where she has a place prepared by God, that they should feed her there one thousand two hundred and sixty days. . . . And the dragon was enraged with the woman, and he went to make war with the rest of her offspring, who keep the commandments of God and have the testimony of Jesus Christ.[13]

Dragon at the Delivery

What a vision—what a woman! Clothed with the resplendent glory of the sun, she stands against the round horizon of space high upon the moon. Pure and bathed in heaven's light, it is very obvious when this woman turns sideways that she is also pregnant! In fact, when we come upon her, she has already gone into labor. Her cries and groans fill the clear air. But so does the salivating roar of an evil dragon, who hungrily crouches before the child-birthing woman, ready to devour her infant the moment he is born.

Who is this terrible dragon? Ah, we should have known—he is "that serpent of old, called the Devil and Satan, who deceives the whole world"![14] And why his voracious appetite for the "male Child" the woman is about to deliver? If the dragon is Satan, then there is no question that the baby Child about to born is none other than the Messiah Himself![15] With a few cryptic strokes of his apocalyptic brush, John hurriedly paints the terrible saga of the dragon's puppet, ancient King Herod, who bloodied Bethlehem in his frantic effort to destroy the Christ child.

But the Child is delivered once again. And the Child becomes a Man. And the Man becomes a Lamb. And the Lamb of God is snatched up to heaven, leaving behind the snapping jaws of a defeated dragon.

Hell hath no fury like a vanquished dragon. Unable to destroy his nemesis the Messiah, the roaring dragon lunges for what He has left behind, the pure and innocent woman who will defend the truth and preserve the kingdom of the Messiah until He returns to earth. The enraged dragon lunges now for her. And she flees. For 1,260 years she trembles in hiding in a wilderness place "prepared by God."

You don't need to be a theologian to quickly pick up John's apocalyptic thread and realize that he is painting the shining portrait of God's friends and Christ's community of faith through the history of Christendom. It is the same dramatic story Daniel's prophecy told in advance—the people of God in the midst of that dark and bloody millennium wherein truth was nearly obliterated by the raging dragon and his earthly puppets. But the woman or the community of faith in Christ was not forgotten by the Man Child who ascended back to heaven. In the midst of dragon wrath, He prepared a place of refuge for this woman. And from that place of hiding she will emerge once again before the end of time to champion the truth of Christ the Messiah.

There she is, Woman Number One in the Apocalypse. The shining symbol of all who "keep the commandments of God and have the testimony of Jesus Christ" to the very end of time.[16]

The Lady Is a Tramp

But there is also Woman Number Two. Let us turn to her canvas now and gaze upon her portrait:

> Then one of the seven angels who had the seven bowls came and talked with me, saying to me, "Come, I will show you the judgment of the great harlot who sits on many waters, with whom the kings of the earth committed fornication, and the inhabitants of the earth were made drunk with the wine of her fornication."
>
> So he carried me away in the Spirit into the wilderness. And I saw a woman sitting on a scarlet beast which was full of names of blasphemy, having seven heads and ten horns. The woman was arrayed in purple and scarlet, and adorned with gold and precious stones and pearls, having in her hand a golden cup full of abominations and the filthiness of her fornication. And on her forehead a name was written: MYSTERY, BABYLON THE GREAT, THE MOTHER OF HARLOTS AND OF THE ABOMINATIONS OF THE EARTH. I saw the woman, drunk with the blood of the saints and with the blood of the martyrs of Jesus. And when I saw her, I marveled with great amazement.[17]

Who in the name of decency is this garish, brazen hussy who defies the God of the universe and sucks the blood of His martyrs? You can almost hear the whistle through the elderly John's teeth and lips as he reels between the stunning portraits of two utterly opposite women! One so pure and pristine, enveloped in the glory of the Son of God. The other so gaudy, so whorish, so inebriated with the blood of the saints—the Lady is a tramp! And it appears the whole world has become intoxicated with her fermented theology and fallen Christianity.

A Blasphemous Claim

The Reformers, to a man, identified this woman to the world. The apocalyptic clues are too evident and too easily identified. "Full of names of blasphemy" is how this canvas paints her. The two definitions of blasphemy in the New Testament leave no doubt as to who this woman might be. In the whisper of the Pharisees, the first definition emerges: "Why does this Man speak blasphemies like this? Who can forgive sins but God alone?"[18] It is blasphemy to claim the prerogative and power of God alone to forgive sins. Any institution or any individual that claims that right has usurped the priesthood of Jesus Christ and corrupted the privilege of God. The second Bible definition of blasphemy is just as clear: "The Jews answered Him, saying, 'For a good work we do not stone You, but for blasphemy, and because You, being a Man, make Yourself God.'"[19] This power, represented by Woman Number Two, would not only claim the prerogative of God to forgive (or refuse to forgive), but she would also make herself as God or goddess before the confused and superstitious masses.

Who is this Woman Number Two? Any careful reading of the history of Christianity and the church will yield to the seeking mind a clarion answer.[20] As we noted in chapter 5, the noble defenders of the faith of Jesus in the great Reformation were neither politically correct nor fuzzily confused regarding the papal identity of this woman called Babylon.

Nor was John confused. Were we to inquire of him these two millennia later, he would be quick to declare: The woman of Revelation 12 represents the pure and true community of faith, and the woman of Revelation 17 represents the corrupted and false community of faith.

So there they are in radical and dramatic contrast—these two symbols of the great dialectic, the dramatic play and counterplay of Revelation: The woman who follows the Lamb—and the woman who rides the beast. The woman who is the handmaiden of Christ—and the woman who is harlot of the Antichrist. The woman who champions the seal of God—and the woman who enforces the mark of the beast. There they are—the two religious communities that shall be embroiled in the final showdown between the Lamb and the Dragon, between Christ and Satan.

There can be no third choice. Because there will be no third camp. Which is precisely why the final question to face every inhabitant of earth will be the choice between the Lamb and the Dragon. Between the shining Lord of the pure woman and the dark lord of the whore.

So what choice have you made?

Before the Clock Runs Out . . .

Here we are—the earth quaking and shaking beneath our feet as a civilization—on this judgment-bound planet here we all are, a judgment-bound society and a judgment-bound people. Every earthquake between this moment and the return of Christ is surely an urgent summons: "Choose you this day—hurry, hurry, don't put it off—choose you this day whom you will serve."[21]

The 144,000 are men and women and young adults and teenagers and children who make their choice. And what is their choice? Mark it and circle it and color it in your own Bible: "These are the ones who follow the Lamb wherever He goes."[22]

To follow the Lamb, to follow the Lord Jesus wherever He goes, wherever He leads. Why shouldn't that be the choice you and I would want to make? Why wouldn't that be the camp you and I would want to join? Because when we make that choice, we make the choice of the 144,000. They choose Jesus. Over Babylon (which means "confusion").

And God knows that our postmodern society is utterly riddled and ruined with confusion. All the giddy late-night laughter in the world cannot salve our moral confusion or staunch our spiritual hemorrhage. The 144,000 may have been in Babylon once upon a time—either ecclesiastically or experientially. But the point is—they have chosen *not* to be defiled by that confusion any longer. They have come out of Babylon now. No more confusion in their lifestyle choices, no more uncertainty in their personal allegiance, no more (as Elijah once cried out) limping back and forth between two camps. Oh, no. They've settled it this time once and for all. It is Jesus they seek, it is Jesus they love, it is Jesus they follow, it is Jesus they serve, it is Jesus they live for and Jesus they will die for if need be. In radical loyalty and humble devotion. Their choices are made, their decision is sealed.

The confession of Nikolaus von Zinzendorf is theirs: "I have but one passion; that is he, only he."

They are the Jesus Generation at the end of time.

"These are the ones who follow the Lamb wherever He goes."[23]

Do you want to join them? I do, too. For as the earth quakes beneath our feet and we hear the tread of an approaching God, now more than ever is the right time to make their choice our own.

"Even so, come, Lord Jesus."

Notes:

[1] Acts 4:31, NKJV. Unless otherwise indicated, all scriptural references in this chapter are from the *New King James Version.*

[2] Revelation 6:12, KJV.

[3] Mike Jones, *Adventist Review,* February 22, 2001.

[4] Luke 21:11, NRSV.

[5] Isaiah 29:6.

[6] Ellen White, *Testimonies for the Church,* vol. 9, p. 97.

[7] Revelation 6:12, 17, KJV, emphasis supplied.

[8] Revelation 7:1-4.

[9] Hebrews 12:22.

[10] Revelation 14:2-5.

[11] Revelation 7:4 describes them as coming from "all the tribes of the children of Israel." But as we learned in chapter 4 of this book, the new Israel of God is no longer bound by geographic borders or ethnic bloodlines. God's new Israel is the community of His friends the world over.

[12] Hebrews 13:4.

[13] Revelation 12:1-6, 17.

[14] Revelation 12:9.

[15] John borrows an ancient messianic phrase from Psalm 2:9 to describe the Child who will "rule all nations with a rod of iron"

[16] Revelation 12:17.

[17] Revelation 17:1-6.

[18]Mark 2:7.

[19]John 10:33.

[20]See my book, *Countdown to the Showdown* (Hart Research Center), where I examine the historical and contemporary evidence that clearly identifies this geo-religio-political power that once again is on the ascendancy on earth.

[21]See Joshua 24:15.

[22]Revelation 14:4.

[23]Revelation 14:4.

Afterword ————————

A FEW FRIDAY EVENINGS AGO my soul was stirred as I read the story of the great English Reformer Hugh Latimer, who was a contemporary of Martin Luther and who, with a cohort of his, was condemned by Bloody Queen Mary to be burned at the stake in 1555.

As the two prelates of the Church of England were being tied to their stake, Latimer turned and spoke to his companion these words now carved on a wall in London: "Be of good comfort, Master Ridley, and play the man: we shall this day light such a candle, by God's grace, in England, as I trust shall never be put out."[1]

My heart bows before such fiery passion for Jesus and His Truth.

And I wonder aloud if the time has not come at last for you and me, too, to "play the man," to "play the woman" for Him. In the gathering gloom of this apocalyptic nightfall, is it not high time that we, too, light such a candle in America that by God's grace shall never be put out?

The two camps of the Apocalypse are, even as I write and as you read, marshaling their forces, strengthening their ranks, identifying their loyal, marking their adherents, defending their positions, preparing their offensive—their final strategic offensive to possess the heart and soul of this last civilization.

This will be truth's finest hour.

And to this hour and to this truth, you and I have been called.

Let us then pray for each other. That the truth of Christ and the courage of Christ might be wedded within our spirits, so that with masters Latimer and Ridley we may yet set ablaze earth's last night.

"Be of good comfort, Master Ridley, and play the man: we shall this day light such a candle, by God's grace, in England, as I trust shall never be put out."

"These are the ones who follow the Lamb wherever He goes."[2]

So let us, too, follow the Lamb, light the candle, and pray the prayer.

"Even so, come, Lord Jesus."

Notes:

[1]L. E. Froom, *The Prophetic Faith of Our Fathers,* vol. 2, p. 370.

[2]Revelation 14:4, NKJV.

Learn more online . . .

What "Left Behind" Left Behind

Study Guides

Follow the link at
www.rusearching.org